Enduring Delight

A Psalm 119 Devotional

Victor R. Scott

The Foundry Press
Columbus, Georgia

Copyright © 2021 Victor R. Scott

Unless otherwise indicated, all scripture quotations are from The Holy Bible, English Standard Version® (ESV®), copyright © 2001 by Crossway, a publishing ministry of Good News Publishers. Used by permission. All rights reserved.

ISBN-13: 978-1-942221-22-7 *(paperback)*
ISBN-13: 978-1-942221-23-4 *(MOBI)*
ISBN-13: 978-1-942221-24-1 *(EPUB)*

An imprint of Scott Publishing Services
Columbus, Georgia

scottpublishingservices@gmail.com

ALL RIGHTS RESERVED. This book contains material protected under International and Federal Copyright Laws and Treaties. Any unauthorized reprint or use of this material is prohibited. No part of this book may be reproduced or transmitted in any form or by any means, electronic or mechanical, including photocopying, recording, or by any information storage and retrieval system without express written permission from the author/publisher.

This book is dedicated to

Drew Anderson

For your friendship has been an enduring delight in my life. Thank you for a constant challenge to think more deeply about what it means to be a Christian.

Table of Contents

Preface 9
Psalm 119:1-4 15
Psalm 119:5-8 19
Psalm 119:9-12 22
Psalm 119:13-16 26
Psalm 119:17-20 30
Psalm 119:21-24 33
Psalm 119:25-28 37
Psalm 119:29-32 40
Psalm 119:33-36 43
Psalm 119:37-40 47
Psalm 119:41-44 50
Psalm 119:45-48 53
Psalm 119:49-52 56
Psalm 119:53-56 59
Psalm 119:57-60 62
Psalm 119:61-64 65
Psalm 119:65-68 69
Psalm 119:69-72 73
Psalm 119:73-76 76

Psalm 119:77-80	79
Psalm 119:81-84	82
Psalm 119:85-88	86
Psalm 119:89-92	90
Psalm 119:93-96	93
Psalm 119:97-100	96
Psalm 119:101-104	100
Psalm 119:105-108	103
Psalm 119:109-112	106
Psalm 119:113-116	109
Psalm 119:117-120	113
Psalm 119:121-124	117
Psalm 119:125-128	120
Psalm 119:129-132	124
Psalm 119:133-136	128
Psalm 119:137-140	131
Psalm 119:141-144	134
Psalm 119:145-148	137
Psalm 119:149-152	140
Psalm 119:153-156	143
Psalm 119:157-160	147
Psalm 119:161-164	151
Psalm 119:165-168	154

Psalm 119:169-172 157
Psalm 119:173-176 160

Preface

Thinking about God and his Word

In the Spring of 2021, I felt led to a journey through the longest psalm in the Bible—Psalm 119. There were two primary reasons. First, the theme of the Psalm is a reflection on the power, purpose, and place of God's word in a believer's life. Since it is written in poetic language, the emotive aspects of the human experience can be woven together with theological insights. The Psalm provided an opportunity to provide both personal reflections on and theological commentary on the text.

The second reason for going through the Psalm was to try and make sense of how we as believers can better engage the revelation of God in the Scriptures. One of the most common approaches to God's word is to treat it like a rule book. While there are commandments we are to obey and learn from, one of the foundational purposes of the Scriptures is to help us know who God is. If we do not know God, we will struggle to know ourselves. This relationship is one of the great mysteries of the Christian faith and journey.

When these reflections were originally written, it was during the liturgical season of Lent. While the content of this book has been modified for publication, there will be some hints of what the season focuses on throughout. This will not take away from material overall, but I felt it was important to note that for you, the reader, from the beginning.

As a brief reminder, during the season of Lent in the Church's calendar, we are encouraged to take time and take a step back and make an assessment of our lives. Where are we going? Is it where we want to go? What could we do to get ourselves refocused on God's purposes for our lives?

This kind of reflection is something we should practice often. But it is not always easy to do. If we are not careful, it could become a time of discouragement rather than growth. The reason being, we are not always good at seeing the big picture. We can very much get distracted by the minutia, the small details, of life.

Great Hope in Difficult Times

Over the course of my life, one of the primary reasons I have remained encouraged in my journey of faith is because I genuinely believe God is sovereign. I believe God has not let go of the steering wheel of this world. Even when it feels like we will go over the cliff, God is still in control.

Now, while some would take this idea of sovereignty to mean God controls every individual facet of the world, we do not need to believe that to trust God's goodness. The miracle of God's oversight over the whole of creation is something we should rejoice in. It can give us comfort and reassurance knowing we are not merely drifting in the cosmos.

We do not have to understand it all. We do not even have to agree with what or how God is doing these things. But, we do need to trust God. This can seem so difficult to do. At least at first.

I have often asked myself why? Why do I struggle to trust God in and through the varied circumstances of life?

I think it has to do with our fear, or at the very least, our reluctance to live a surrendered life to God.

Our desire to maintain control over what we cannot control is more damaging than we know. And what are we trying to control, you may be asking? We are trying to control outcomes. But that is not for us to decide. It is beyond our power. We must live our lives the best we can with the information we have available to us at the moment we are making our decisions.

We do not know, and we cannot know, how any individual choice will turn out. But we can decide how we will respond regardless of the outcome.

Our attitude, to a degree not often considered, determines how well we live.

A Season of Reflection

As I mentioned earlier, the reflections in the book were written during Lent, a penitential time in the Church's calendar. What this means is that during this season, we seek to refocus our lives. We should strive to identify those attitudes and habits that are getting in the way of our spiritual growth.

One of the great underappreciated disciplines of the Christian journey is reflection. For those of us who did not grow up in a liturgical church, the ebb and flow of the Church Calendar can seem strange. And yet, as the years have passed, I have found this steady rhythm comforting and enlightening. In particular, the regular reminder to think on what it means to obey God, follow Jesus, and follow the Holy Spirit's promptings.

The Word of the Lord

In the summer of 2019, I was introduced and began to immerse myself in the study of the Book of Common Prayer tradition. And while there are other traditions in the Christian family, this particular form has been of particular encouragement and challenge to me. I have been encouraged by the simple pattern of prayer I am offered as I pray the Daily Office. I have been encouraged by the thought that there are millions of other Christians praying in similar, if not identical ways. I have been encouraged by the effect it has had on and in my life.

But I have also been challenged. As we read the scriptures, either corporately when we gather for worship or individually in private devotion, there is a short call-and-response we participate in. It is a reminder that God's word is not merely a religious text. The Scriptures are a means of communication, from the mind of God to our hearts. In the short exchange, the leader declares the scriptures appointed and at the end of the reading says to the congregation, "The Word of the Lord." The people then respond, "Thanks be to God."

What has been so challenging about this short exchange is how it reminds me that the word of God has been spoken, and I, if I am being attentive, have heard words that proceeded from the mind of God. In other words, when I hear the Scriptures read aloud, or when I read them during my times of prayer, God is again saying something through those words that is specifically for me. As a child of God, I am being blessed by those words that God spoke and preserved in the collected Scriptures of the Old and New Testaments.

What a wonderful gift!

The Word on the Way

It is with this in mind that I want to draw our attention to the focus of this book.

Not only is Psalm 119 the longest Psalm, but its particular focus is on the way the Word of God is to operate in the life of those who seek, serve, and submit to

God. This is what makes it an important Psalm to consider and meditate on.

My hope and prayer are that as we consider what the Psalmist wrote, we will see through the Psalm like a lens. And as we peer through the images and illustrations offered to us, we will understand more deeply what God is calling us to.

May our conviction be that the Word of God is what we need not just at the rest stops of life, but as we live and as we continue to walk in the way of the Lord.

May our love for God lead us to a deeper commitment and more faithful obedience as we come to know the sweet savor and enduring delight of his Word.

Psalm 119:1-4

¹ Blessed are those whose way is blameless,
   who walk in the *law of the Lord!* ¹
² Blessed are those who keep *his testimonies*,
   who seek him with their whole heart,
³ who also do no wrong, but walk
   in *his ways!*
⁴ You have commanded *your precepts* to
   be kept diligently.

Reflection

The life of the believer in Jesus will be marked by one important choice: will I strive to live according to the will of God as contained in the word of God.

This may feel like an oversimplification. And it might be. But the benefit of thinking about our journey in these terms is that it clarifies what the goal actually is. Whether we are comfortable with it yet or not, we must

---

[1] *Those phrases that identify God's word, revelation, or law in some form will be highlighted in the text in the hopes of accentuating the many and varied ways we can visualize what God has given to us for our good.*

live in such a way that when we stand before our Lord and Savior we hear him say, "Well done."

One of the great realizations of my life in Christ was discovering that what God commands are the training wheels of faith. They are not the end of faith. They are not the totality of faith. They are the beginning. What God calls us to do in obedience is what trains us to go deeper into who he is and what he has called us to be in the world.

The more I think about this, the more profound the realization. And the more clear the task.

Commentary

Verse 1: There is a link between the integrity of our lives and the state of blessedness we experience. But what is it that bridges these two realities? The inference from the text is that it is a commitment to our obedience to "the law of the Lord." This phrase is a shorthand for the whole of God's revelation. For that which God has spoken and left for our edification in the written Scriptures. To be blessed and to be seen as blameless and to walk in the law of the Lord are not disconnected ideas. They are, in fact, the way we know we are moving in the same direction as God.

Verse 2: What does it mean to "keep his testimonies"? To treasure. To esteem. To protect because of what it means to us. Does this define our disposition for what God has said about himself? What others have said about him? Too often we make the mistake of thinking that "knowing" is the same as "keeping." It is not. The former speaks to a mere familiarity with or an awareness of something. The latter to a deep and abiding intimacy. And this is a key to making sense of why we ought to keep his testimonies. In our pursuit of God, we do it with our "whole heart." With the totality of who we are. We are not merely trying to find God. We are trying to connect with God. To be known by God in the deepest of ways.

Verse 3: The pursuit and the treasuring inferred in verse 2 manifests itself in a life that embodies the essence and character of God. We "do no wrong." We are increasingly able to discern what we ought to do, for that is most pleasing to God. And, in our pleasing God, we are deeply fulfilled. Satisfied in our innermost being. As we discover what God requires of us, we can see the manner of our living is changed. It is transformed. So much so that we begin to walk like he walks. We are more than just copying his actions. Our apprehension of what it means to be with God and to be like God matures. It grows clearer in our ability to understand how we are supposed to live. We then recognize how we are becoming living examples of God's grace.

Verse 4: The kind of life that is blessed and has internalized the truths of the law of the Lord is a disciplined life. I find that we take exception far too quickly with God's commands. Why should we not listen to the one voice that has our best interests at heart and who knows the end from the beginning? Why do we buck so strongly that instruction? Is it because we fail to accept that in our own limitations we will fail more often than we care to admit? The apostle John tells us that the commands of God are not burdensome (1 John 5:3). And yet many seem to feel as though they are being overwhelmed by what has been requested. We must confront this tendency. We have been commanded to be diligent in our keeping of God's precepts. That requires discipline and trust in God to do with confidence.

Psalm 119:5-8

⁵ Oh that my ways may be steadfast
　in keeping *your statutes*!
⁶ Then I shall not be put to shame,
　having my eyes fixed on
　all *your commandments*.
⁷ I will praise you with an upright heart,
　when I learn *your righteous rules*.
⁸ I will keep *your statutes*; do not
　utterly forsake me!

Reflection

The life of faith is mired with possibilities. It can feel at times that there are too many options for how God may want us to go. The uncomfortable irony is that there are not as many "options" as we may think. But there are a good many we have not even considered. This has, unfortunately, become a convenient excuse to avoid taking any action. Fear has more to do with our inaction than a lack of direction.

God is only interested in one thing, that we would live a life that is consistent with his character. This is why in our search to live this out, we can find ourselves struggling to find out which of the many ways of expressing that singular reality we should pursue. Each opportunity is unique as our imaginations can create. Therefore, we should not be quick to choose or to quit looking.

What I have found out in the last few years is that by increasing my focus on becoming more like God, I am able to have a wider impact. Not because I am trying to, but because I am available to. The closer I grow in my relationship with God, the easier it is to hear what he wants of me. The clearer I see the world the way he does.

All of this begins with a commitment to keep our "eyes fixed on all [his] commandments."

Commentary

Verse 5: The first section of Psalm 119 concludes with a cry for strength in daily obedience. The idea of being "steadfast" points to a firmness of conviction. It carries the implication of resolution and of not being swayed or deterred. The Psalmist calls upon the Lord to fortify them because the tendency will be to not remain steadfast. The precepts of the Lord are contrary to the current of the world around us, therefore it requires an increased commitment to persist in our obedience as God rightly deserves to receive.

Verse 6: How does the Psalmist characterize the effect of remaining steadfast in God's precepts? We see the answer here in verse 6. When we are steadfast, we are not then "put to shame." This is not about embarrassment or fear. To be put to shame points more to living according to a lie. To being exposed as frauds and charlatans. The more resolute the strength of our conviction to obey God's word, the greater our confidence in God himself. This is an odd relationship. But only when we do not consider God's commands to be perfect. For God to expect complete obedience, we must believe in the complete and total goodness of God. That he will not call us to an action that will purposely lead us to evil or ruin.

Verse 7: The greater our commitment to learn and apply what God has instructed, the greater its impact on our hearts. We become more like God because we are conforming ourselves to his character. This will inevitably lead to praise. To worship. When we know God better, by living as he lives, we grow in our ability to draw near to him.

Verse 8: The closing verse of the first section is a plea. The Psalmist offers a promise to "keep your statutes". They then ask for God to remain faithful to them. The sentiment is quite passionate. "Do not *utterly* forsake me!" (Emphasis added). It is not necessarily that the Psalmist fears being cast off from God, but rather that there is a recognition that in keeping the Lord's statutes there is a corresponding promise by God to be attentive to their plight.

Psalm 119:9-12

⁹ How can a young man keep his way pure?
  By guarding it according to *your word*.
¹⁰ With my whole heart I seek you; let me
  not wander from *your commandments*!
¹¹ I have stored up *your word* in my heart,
  that I might not sin against you.
¹² Blessed are you, O Lord;
  teach me *your statutes*!

Reflection

One of the great fears of the Christian journey is failing to live up to God's standard of holiness. Well, allow me to comfort you my friends. No one can live up to that standard. There is not a single person who has ever lived who has matched God's perfect standard; other than Jesus.

This is a wonderfully uncomfortable truth to accept. We are not perfect. And we will never be perfect as we travel on life's road. What we can do, what we should strive to achieve is a steady progress in our understanding of God's goodness. This is what will produce the transformative effect we should see.

When we live our lives with God, and others, in fear of failure, we actually rob ourselves of one of the essential comforts of our relationship with God. The issue is not whether or not we will fail, the issue is whether not we can accept being accepted by God in spite of our failures.

When we try to manage God's expectations of us we are robbing ourselves of experiencing God's grace. Whether we fully appreciate it or not, the reality is that our constant trying to impress God actually short-circuits our spiritual development. The focus shifts from relationship to regulations, from love to performance, and from grace to works.

The word of God, his commandments and statutes serve as the guard rails of life. They are what keep us from veering off into unhealthy directions. What's more, when we realize this function of God's word, we may very well stop trying to be God, and simply enjoy being his children. We can trust God's direction and even God's boundaries for our lives when we accept and surrender to his tender care. And this care is seen best when we obey his commands more.

Commentary

Verse 9: The second section of Psalm 119 begins with a simple question. This question reflects the often unspoken struggle of God's people: how can we keep our way pure? In other words, how can we please God with our lives? The answer is simple and puzzling. It is simple in that we are given one task. We are to "guard" our way. This means that there will be assaults against our living in purity. There will be circumstances that would pull us away from where we should be and what we should do. But there is something puzzling about this task. The Psalmist implies that there is an attribute to God's word that makes guarding our way possible. That characteristic is that God's word is the codification of God's wisdom. When God speaks, we should listen. When we listen, we can learn. And if we learn, we can live in a way that is pleasing to God.

Verse 10: We see here, the link between intentional devotion and a focused life. The Psalmist makes it clear that we ought to fill our hearts completely with the labor of seeking after God. To seek is to pursue. To commit ourselves to find what we are searching for. In the Christian journey we should avoid taking a passive posture toward God. While God's presence is everywhere, his focus is drawn to our yearning for him. When we seek, he draws near. But our seeking is to be directed by his commandments. As we heed them and obey them we are kept on track. Our course through life is safeguarded by God's word. Why? Because God's word will always return to God and will never be empty. Look at what God said through the Prophet Isaiah, "...so shall my word be that goes out from my mouth; it shall not return to me empty, but it shall accomplish that which I purpose, and shall succeed in the thing for which I sent it" (Isaiah 55:11 ESV).

Verse 11: Continuing with the theme of the heart, the Psalmist declares that the word of God can be "stored up." We do not often think about the fact that the word is not a limited resource. It is bountiful and rich. We can return to it over and over and draw from it new strength. The reservoir of God's word never runs dry. But why should we store up God's word? These resources are what we use to fight against sin in our lives. When we have God's word in our heart, we eliminate the room for sin to get in. This is not a formula. It is a process. The more of God's word that is in us, the less room exists for anything else.

Verse 12: The Psalmist takes a moment to worship and honor God. We must bless the Lord. Not with some physical gift. God has no need for anything material. When we bless God, we are acting and living with the correct knowledge of who and what God is. To do anything less is to not bless the Lord. Interestingly, it is in the context of worship that the Psalmist petitions the Lord to instruct them in God's statutes. Our desire to learn should not be seen as separated from our worship of God. The greater our worship, the more our capacity to be taught increases. It may seem paradoxical, but that does not negate the implication of this relationship between worship and instruction.

Psalm 119:13-16

¹³ With my lips I declare all *the rules of your mouth*.
¹⁴ In the way of *your testimonies* I delight as much as in all riches.
¹⁵ I will meditate on *your precepts* and fix my eyes on *your ways*.
¹⁶ I will delight in *your statutes*; I will not forget *your word*.

Reflection

There is a famous phrase attributed to the great St. Francis of Assisi.

> "Preach the Gospel at all times.
> When necessary, use words."
> St. Francis of Assisi
> (*Attributed*)

The problem is, there is no concrete evidence that he actually said this. Well, maybe calling it a problem is a bit much. It would be more accurate to say that this refrain may actually be a summary or restatement of his actual thoughts. It is possible that this pithier version was distilled from what St. Francis actually said, namely: "It is no use walking anywhere to preach unless our walking is our preaching."[2]

The reason for considering this idea from St. Francis is, it helps us understand that as we learn more of God's word, we can begin to have our thoughts shaped and reshaped by God's thoughts.

As we spend time with God, we are influenced and directed in ways that actually bring us closer to where God is drawing us.

Whether we know it or not, the manner in which we live our lives does have an impact in how others receive what we say to them. There needs to be a congruence between word and action. However, and this is just as important, we can't avoid speaking what we know to be true just because we are still figuring out how to live in greater consistency!

I find that, too often, I don't speak because of some fear of being seen as a hypocrite. But this happens when what we say is coming from us. When we are the source. But if we are speaking the words of God, it doesn't matter if I'm saying it or some donkey on the road. The words of God are true even when a notorious liar speaks them.

---

[2] https://www.huffpost.com/entry/preach-the-gospel-at-all-times-st-francis_b_1627781

They may be the only true things that person ever says. But that doesn't make the words any less true.

As we invest time in God's word, and as we inwardly digest that word in our lives, the greater our assurance of faith with God. And as we grow in grace, we must share what we have learned, even when we haven't fully implemented what God has said.

Commentary

Verse 13: There is a sense in which we will never fulfill the charge of this verse. But that is not its intent. By making this declaration, the Psalmist is displaying the nature of what our commitment should be. There is an intentionality to the work of proclaiming the rules of God. But the breadth of this commitment is to declare "all the rules." We cannot select which rules we like and then discard the rest. If we take up the mantle of heralding the rules of God, we must faithfully declare them all. From the most glorious to the most convicting. To speak one is to become responsible for speaking them all.

Verse 14: The comparison described here is shocking. The gladness that comes from having the security of riches, of having the stability that material wealth can afford is compared to the delighting in God's testimonies. What God says can comfort and heal and encourage and instruct. To have God's testimonies is to be protected. We do not have to shun material blessings.

But we must not diminish the purpose and power of what God has spoken in the Scriptures.

Verse 15: We have been reminded several times in the Psalm to develop a focused attention on God's ways. In this verse we are encouraged to meditate. This is another way of describing the spending of time to reflect on what God has given to us. It is the intentional mulling over of the precept we are considering. To use a culinary idea, to meditate is to marinate in the precept we are contemplating. To allow the truth we are engaging to get inside of us, flavoring us with its attributes. As we meditate, we are also to once again look upon God's example. God's ways are not our ways (Isaiah 55:8), but we must strive to conform our lives to them anyway.

Verse 16: This is another reference to delight. In this case, the delight is directed at the statutes of God themselves. The reality of how God's words and commands can bring joy to our lives can be somewhat counterintuitive, but it is important to consider. In order to achieve it, we have to understand God's commands as a gift rather than a restriction, as a key rather than a lock. The Psalmist continues by offering a statement of conviction: "I will not forget your word." In order to not forget, something must first be known.

Psalm 119:17-20

¹⁷ Deal bountifully with your servant, that I
    may live and keep *your word*.
¹⁸ Open my eyes, that I may behold
    wondrous things out of *your law*.
¹⁹ I am a sojourner on the earth; hide not
    your commandments from me!
²⁰ My soul is consumed with longing for
    your rules at all times.

Reflection

The power of the word to transform and set free cannot be easily described. But once it has been experienced, it can never be denied. We can become discouraged when we do not see the kind of transformation we desire. It can create doubt and even fear that we will be consigned to the uncertainty of not knowing if God is pleased with us.

We do not have to live with this cloud of anxiety. There is a promise we can hold on to.

God desires for us to live with him according to the truth. That is why he gave us his word. That we might learn it and be transformed by it. When we interact with God's word, we are awakened to more than we could ever have imagined.

The promise we have is that if we desire to see, God can give us the ability. But we have to actually want to see. We have to accept the implications and ramifications of what that means.

In our search for God, we will discover more than we may have ever wanted to admit about ourselves. This is the price we pay to have an honest and true relationship with God.

Commentary

Verse 17: The desire of the Psalmist is to live in such a way that they might live out God's word. In order to accomplish this, the writer asks God to bless them. To bestow upon them an abundance of blessing so they may live out what God has spoken. Now, it would be easy to think this is a request for material blessing. However, that would not fit the context. What the Psalmist needs and what God can provide in infinite quantities is the spiritual fervor to obey his commands. This perspective would be a more accurate way of understanding the request.

Verse 18: A second request in this section is for the Lord to give the Psalmist the ability to see. This kind of sight is what we all should desire. It is the ability we need to perceive the world as God made it and wants it to be. Without this divine sight, we will experience severe difficulty on our journey of faith. What makes this second request particularly interesting is the Psalmist's reason for asking. That they might see "the wondrous things out of your law." The inference here is there are wondrous things that we should see in God's law that we often do not see. When we are unable to see those things, there is a gap in our understanding of what God has revealed.

Verse 19: The journey of life is transient. Those who live for any length of time will see the effects and impact of death. Seeing our time on earth as a period where we are "passing through" can be helpful. It can force us to consider how we expend our energy and what consumes our time. We are journeying through. We will not be here forever. In light of this transient reality, the Psalmist asks God to provide access to his commandments. To not hide them for us. In our knowledge of God's commands there is information that makes this journey easier to navigate.

Verse 20: What we value is what we dedicate our time and efforts to. The writer here explicitly states their soul is "consumed with longing for [God's] rules." Let us take this declaration at face value. The intensity of this conviction exposes the singular focus all followers of Christ should desire. Faith is not, or ought not to be, something we turn off and on. Who we are in God because of the work of Christ should be the defining reality of our lives.

Psalm 119:21-24

²¹ You rebuke the insolent, accursed ones,
   who wander from *your commandments*.
²² Take away from me scorn and
   contempt, for I have kept
   your testimonies.
²³ Even though princes sit plotting
   against me, your servant will
   meditate on *your statutes*.
²⁴ *Your testimonies* are my delight; they are
   my counselors.

Reflection

It only takes one day of living to know that not all is well in the world. The brokenness of the human experience is manifested in a myriad of ways. They do not all have to be named, to be known. They hover over our minds like a fog that never lifts. This is the dark side of life.

In the verses that serve as our focus today, we see the heaviness of the fall. We see it in the struggle of living apart from God's word. We see the barrage that we must face even when we have been faithful to what God has instructed. The injustices we may be forced to endure when we have no access to the means of relief. These and so many more could rob us of our ability to rejoice in God. If we would let them.

But the Psalmist calls us to a deeper wisdom. One grounded in the testimonies of God where delight springs with an unquenchable constancy. There is a form of wisdom the world offers to us, but it will fail. And the reason it will do so is it cannot replenish itself. It will always be short-sighted because it comes from those whose vision is marred.

The wisdom of God can penetrate the darkness of the world. No shadow can restrain its brilliance. No corner can hide from its influence. There is nothing that can dampen the power of God's wisdom. That is why we can rest in it. And why our confidence will never be misplaced.

Commentary

Verse 21: To "wander from [God's] commandments" is the surest way of incurring the discipline of God. Not because God will actively bring his rebuke. The reality is any move away from what God has given for us to do will invariably result in discipline. In our obedience we receive the blessing of God's protection. But in our disobedience, we say to God we do not need his loving care. This is why our wandering can be so dangerous. God does not desire or enjoy the discipline of his children. But God has already given us the way of escape. We are the ones who must take it.

Verse 22: One of the difficulties most often associated with obedience will be the disdain of those who are not in relationship with God. Our desire to submit to God and live in accord with his testimonies identify us to the world. We must not be surprised by this. In fact, we should expect it. However, we do not have to enjoy this kind of suffering. We can call upon the Lord to provide a reprieve. We can look to our God and inquire for relief from these burdens. But, even if they are not removed, we should not allow those discomforts and frustrations to impede us from keeping God's word.

Verse 23: It does not matter who may find reason to come against us, their station in life should not become a distraction to how we live our faith before God. If there is one thing that is certain on our journey of faith it is that we will encounter opposition. It may not be another person necessarily. But whatever it may be, we must do all we can to not be distracted or deterred. When we meditate on God's statutes, we are striving to focus our attention on what God has directed us to do. This cannot happen when our minds are drawn away from what we are trying to contemplate.

Verse 24: We again encounter the Psalmist speaking of delighting in God's words. This reminder is vital if we are going to understand how we should feel about God's commands. They should not feel like burdens to us (1 John 5:3). They are to be for our minds and souls a refreshing ointment and a healing balm. To approach God's word as an inconvenience is to not fully appreciate their role in our lives. This way of understanding God's words takes time to understand, and even longer to cultivate. But this should be the charge we take up each and every day.

Psalm 119:25-28

²⁵ My soul clings to the dust; give me life
  according to *your word*!
²⁶ When I told of my ways, you answered
  me; teach me *your statutes*!
²⁷ Make me understand the way of
  your precepts, and I will meditate
  on your *wondrous works*.
²⁸ My soul melts away for sorrow;
  strengthen me according to *your word*!

Reflection

It would be tempting to think we can endure the journey of life with less of God's word. The terrible irony is this: without God's word we are wandering in an endless desert with no source of water within reach. The word of God is the portable oasis we need to survive our travels in this world. And it has been given to us as a heavenly gift.

When we tap into the totality of God's commands, we receive the fullness of its provision. This does not mean we are actualizing all that God has provided. It is better to say we have access to it all, and as we mature and grow in wisdom, we enjoy the benefits more intentionally.

God's word can be what leads us to safety, or it can feel like a millstone around our necks. How we experience it will depend on why we engage with it. If we approach God's word as a gift, we find security and counsel. If we approach God's word as a burden, we will feel the weight of all we have been forgiven of by Christ's redemptive work on the Cross.

It took me a long time to see this. And now that I know it, I can never go back to how things used to be. Knowing and living in God's good pleasure is not worth surrendering, for any reason. Under any circumstances.

Commentary

Verse 25: How did God create all things? In the opening chapter of the Bible, we are told that he spoke them into existence. By the power of his word what never existed came into being. While not to the same degree, the word of God as contained in the Scriptures continues to infuse life in all who embrace God's word. Why? Because the word of God written comes from the same source as the words of God spoken. When we read God's commandments, their power is not resident on the pages, but in the author. The author is the one who validates and enacts the Truths the words on the page convey.

Verse 26: The God who has spoken (and continues to speak) desires for us to be vocal as well. The apostle

Paul captured this idea when he asked, "And how are they to hear without someone preaching?" (Romans 10:14 ESV). The preacher is the mouthpiece of God, carrying the words of God, to those who need to hear from God. We reflect our heavenly Father best when we imitate him in being verbal communicators. We don't have to speak to thousands to do this. Sometimes our audience need only be one person. And, in order to speak, the Psalmist asks God to teach them.

Verse 27: The Psalmist makes a link between our understanding of God's precepts and our desire to consider the "wondrous works" of God. We do not always understand how studying God's word, how reflecting on what God has revealed helps us to appreciate his labors in the world. The Psalmist in another place tells us that the heavens declare the glory of God (Psalm 19:1 ESV). How? By reminding us that all beautiful things come into being by the hand of an artist.

Verse 28: The struggles of life can feel overwhelming. We are reminded of this here. The imagery is that of the soul melting away. Our endurance will be taxed in this world. Adversity will be a companion to everyone at some point in their lives. The question is how do we find the strength to persevere? We are told that it is found in God's word. There is a property in God's word that can invigorate us even in the midst of strife. Into this reality we must entrust ourselves. For when we do, we will experience a renewal of courage.

Psalm 119:29-32

²⁹ Put false ways far from me and
 graciously teach me *your law!*
³⁰ I have chosen the way of faithfulness; I
 set *your rules* before me.
³¹ I cling to *your testimonies,* O Lord; let me
 not be put to shame!
³² I will run in the way of *your
 commandments* when you
 enlarge my heart!

Reflection

It is often the case that we make decisions based on incomplete information. And it is also true, we will not always have the amount of information we would like. The consequence of this is we may never really feel confident in what we decide. We struggle to minimize all of the possible negative outcomes, only to find out we missed something in our assessments.

As we continue living with God, we will discover that perfect wisdom is not something we can ever attain. But, we don't have too. If our trust is in God and our hope in Christ, we can rely on them to lead us where we should go. There is no need to try and "figure it all out." We can seek the Lord and he can direct our steps.

Our hope cannot be built on what we know. We will never know enough. If we can turn over that desire to God, we may just discover God is all we will ever need to navigate through life. Let's rejoice in God's wisdom as he has given it to us in his word.

Commentary

Verse 29: The contrast between "false ways" and being instructed in God's law is a helpful reminder. The deeper our understanding of God's law, the easier it becomes to fend off the temptation to believe falsehoods. The Psalmist writes this in the form of a supplication. By framing their request in this way, we learn how we will continually need God's assistance. We cannot manage the many ways we can be drawn to what is untrue. We cannot anticipate all of the avenues whereby we may encounter a lie. We therefore need help. And it is right and prudent to seek it.

Verse 30: Here the Psalmist declares a decision of how they will live before and with God. They describe this as "the way of faithfulness." What a fitting description of how we should strive to live. We are on a journey. But we do not know how long we will be traveling. So, it is wise to make a clear commitment to endure until we have arrived. What we should avoid, as much as we can, is not enjoying the journey itself. And we do that by allowing God's "rules" to serve as a guide. As we grow in our trust of what God has said, the greater our confidence that we are on the right path.

Verse 31: When the circumstances of life would rob us of joy, and the unexpected obstacles we may have to traverse try to discourage us, we should "cling to [God's] testimonies." And why should we make a habit of doing this? Because when we do, we position ourselves to be aided by God's good mercy. As we labor to grow in our understanding of what God has said, the better our ability to see what God is doing. But something else happens. The clearer our memories of God's past interventions become. We may not always see it, but God has been present.

Verse 32: This is a simple, and yet beautiful, encouragement here. As we interact and internalize God's word, our stamina for obedience increases. We will no longer merely walk in God's commandment. We will be able to run. To advance even faster on the journey toward maturity. And the reason we will have this increased capacity is because God will have enlarged our hearts. Our awareness and sensitivity to God's movement in our lives will then become easier to identify as a result.

Psalm 119:33-36

³³ Teach me, O Lord, the way of *your statutes*; and I will keep it to the end.
³⁴ Give me understanding, that I may keep *your law* and observe it with my whole heart.
³⁵ Lead me in the path of *your commandments*, for I delight in it.
³⁶ Incline my heart to *your testimonies*, and not to selfish gain!

Reflection

There is no greater teacher than God. He knows the end from the beginning. He founded the heavens and the earth so that they would sustain life. In his eternal wisdom God has arranged all we see and all we have yet to see. It is within this context, with this level of access that God offers to lead us. What's more, God invites us to seek his mind that we might conform our lives to it.

Over the years I have wondered why the Church continues to relitigate some issues and topics. It seems we never really get ahead of them. Could it be we have not really sought God's wisdom on these things? The work of theological reflection can become so complicated. I think it is because of pride. We want to be the ones who discover "the key" that gives us the power or influence or insight we all need. This will never happen.

Whether we want to admit it or not, whether we want to accept it or not, God has already given to us the instrument, means, and strategy for addressing all that is wrong with the world. And that includes starting with me.

If we are not satisfied with God's answers on the subjects that cause us concern, why do we think another flawed, broken, and sinful person's answer will be any consolation? It will not be. It cannot be. And until we come to terms with this, we will seek other teachers other than God. We will seek other saviors other than Jesus. We will rely on other means of support other than the Holy Spirit.

As a Christian, anyone who offers you a solution that does not begin with, is saturated by, and terminates in Jesus is selling you something that will not last. More to the point, it will fail to accomplish its alleged purpose.

Commentary

Verse 33: The Psalmist petitions the Lord to teach them God's statutes. This is an invitation to greater responsibility. We may not always understand instruction in this way, but within the context of our relationship with God, it is precisely this. The greater our knowledge of God, the higher God's expectation of our obedience. The more we know, the more we become accountable for. And, as a result we understand why there is value in continuing to learn and grow and obey.

Verse 34: Because the law of God originated in the mind of God, there are aspects of it for which we require God's assistance to understand. This does not necessarily mean we could not figure it out if we had all the time in the world. The problem is that we don't have the time! What God knows by virtue of his being God, creates an insurmountable obstacle to us, if it were not for God's gracious intervention. The theological concept that describes this process is: Revelation. God must reveal what we could not discover through our own efforts, but once it has been provided, we can see what was intended.

Verse 35: The commandments of God, in one sense, serve to clear the road in front of us. What this means is as we more clearly understand God's laws, we grow in wisdom. As we grow in wisdom, our ability to see further down the road of life also increases. Maturity, whether in the natural or the spirit, has a way of bringing peace of mind. And when we are able to rightly determine a course of action, we can enjoy the fruit of those insights. The primary fruit, which is delight, according to the writer.

Verse 36: One of the best antidotes to selfishness is surrender to God's testimonies. Seeing and knowing how God has worked has a way of focusing our attention. When our attention is God, we do not have time to focus on anything else. This distracted living, where we have time to look at what others have or are doing, can lead us down paths of selfishness we never intended or thought possible.

Psalm 119:37-40

³⁷ Turn my eyes from looking at worthless
things; and give me life in *your ways*.
³⁸ Confirm to your servant *your promise*,
that you may be feared.
³⁹ Turn away the reproach that I dread, for
your rules are good.
⁴⁰ Behold, I long for *your precepts*; in your
righteousness give me life!

Reflection

There are as many opportunities for distraction in the world as there are sets of eyes. This is one of the many unspoken challenges to living a life that is in accord with God's word.

We have to choose to turn our eyes and our attention toward God. To refocus our efforts and to submit our impulses to the will of God does not come cheaply. A cost will be incurred. Too often I find myself hoping God will simply make living by faith easier. And then I am confronted with an even more pressing realization, how does that help me become stronger? It doesn't.

As the years have passed and I have seen more of what this world has to offer (both good and bad), my confidence in God's commands has grown. I want to trust the all-wise God to lead me. To comfort me through his immovable faithfulness.

In a world where everything appears to be in flux, the notion of an immovable God can be disorienting. And yet, this reality is our safe harbor. It is our calm in the storm. Because God never moves, we can always find him to be right where he has promised. And that place is where he has always been, for he is the ever-present God. There is no place where he is not, for there is no place where he cannot be.

Commentary

Verse 37: Sometimes we need help averting our eyes from those things that would draw our attention from God. We would like to believe we have the spiritual maturity and strength to do it on our own. However, this is not often the case. As we turn away from those "worthless things," we can turn to God. And as we turn to him, we can call upon God to give us life. But this life is not on our terms. It is life in God's ways. This is neither unreasonable nor should it be surprising.

Verse 38: When those moments of doubt come, and they will, we can ask God for a reminder. There are promises God makes that appear too big to believe. They just don't seem possible. When the reality of what God has promised begins to sink in, then comes the doubt and worry. How can we keep from ruining the precious gift God has given? We may be tempted to think this way, but we should reject this line of thought. Whatever God promises he will fulfill. And there is nothing more praiseworthy than a person who keeps their word. So, when God makes a promise, both of blessing and discipline, we should listen and heed his word.

Verse 39: The Psalmist says that God's "rules are good." This is not simple lip service. This is a declaration of an inherent quality of God's word that must be reclaimed. What God has commanded is good. Period. And the tension is often felt is our rejection of this particular good. When we know what we ought to do and choose another path, we instinctively feel the reproach of the decision. It is a willful rejection of something God has given. Something good God has provided for our comfort and direction.

Verse 40: The life we have in Christ originated in God's righteousness. Another way of thinking about God's righteousness is as God's essence. That quality of being that defines how God operates. God is good. He is righteous. Therefore, he will never act in a way contrary to these immutable realities. As followers of Christ and believers in God, we can walk in God's precepts because we can count on God's unchanging character.

Psalm 119:41-44

⁴¹ Let your steadfast love come to me,
   O Lord, your salvation according
   to *your promise*;
⁴² then shall I have an answer for him who
   taunts me, for I trust in *your word*.
⁴³ And take not the word of truth utterly
   out of my mouth, for my hope is in
   your rules.
⁴⁴ I will keep *your law* continually,
   forever and ever,

Reflection

If the Bible is the word of God (and I believe that it is) and if God is all wise (and again, I believe that he is), then when we study and internalize its truth we too become wise. Not to the same degree as God, but definitely in the same direction.

The world pretends to offer us wisdom. It boasts of its own insights and revelations. To the average person these ideas can seem interesting and can even stimulate our curiosity. The problem is none of this moves us closer to God. In the end, the wisdom of the world is a dead end.

One of the deflections the world tries to get us, those who claim to follow Christ, to accept is that it is a form of wisdom equal in quality as that of God's. On its face, this notion is ridiculous. But, too many in the Church have bought into the lie. This is not the way of truth and light.

If we desire to live in a way congruent with God's character, then we must do all we can to know what God actually desires and commands. Fortunately for us, God has provided us with access to this information. It is found in his Word. And when we engage with it and allow ourselves to be molded by it, we will become wiser than the world could ever dream.

Commentary

Verse 41: There is a symmetry to the clauses in this verse. In particular, there is a synonymous relationship between God's steadfast love and his salvation. The Psalmist asks for God's love to come to them. And in the following clause there is a further description of what that love is. It is the salvation God gives because of God's promise. When we think of God's love, we are also looking at what that love has provided, namely salvation.

Verse 42: The approaching of God's love, the experiencing of God's salvation is the answer we have against those who would deride us. When we are mocked and ridiculed, our answer is that we are loved by God and we are saved because of God's faithful promise. Our answer to the opposition we face is found in the word we have grown to trust. This is one aspect of God's word often overlooked. Until we understand how God's word gives us the answers to our detractors, we will struggle to trust it to provide the answers we yearn for in other areas of life.

Verse 43: When we know the value and power of God's "word of truth," we will understand how much we need it. It becomes more than just a means of instruction, it becomes our support in times of great stress and distress. We can find our hope because of what God has said in his word, and through his commands God points to the greater reality of his care and affection. When we finally and completely appreciate what we have, we dread the thought of its absence.

Verse 44: The final verse of this section is a vow. The Psalmist vows to keep God's law "continually." The idea here is of a dedicated observance. The person who accepts the authority of God's word in their lives also accepts the commitment it will take to stay true to it. That is not to say there will not be days of struggle and moments of doubt. The nature of a vow is to serve as a reminder to the one who made it that they are now under a particular obligation. An obligation they entered into freely.

Psalm 119:45-48

⁴⁵ and I shall walk in a wide place, for I
 have sought *your precepts*.
⁴⁶ I will also speak of *your testimonies* before
 kings and shall not be put to shame,
⁴⁷ for I find my delight in *your
 commandments*, which I love.
⁴⁸ I will lift up my hands toward *your
 commandments*, which I love, and I will
 meditate on *your statutes*.

Reflection

An often underappreciated effect of God's word in our lives is the development of courage. We don't always make this connection. I think this is the case because we interact with God's commandment in search of answers, rather than in search of wisdom.

The difference between answers and wisdom is that answers resolve one question. But wisdom prepares us to answer a variety of questions. When we become wise we learn to adapt and adjust. It is this ability that gives us greater courage. We no longer fear not having answers because we have learned how to find solutions.

This courage then makes us more resilient. We worry less about not being able to stand for what we believe. Or about what others will say to us or about us. Courage is a quality belonging to those who know themselves. And, it is a characteristic of those who trust in God more than in their own strength.

When we have been formed by God's wisdom, there are few challenges we have to fear.

Commentary

Verse 45: The idea of walking in a "wide place" leaves the impression of a multitude of options. There are many avenues that could be taken, but because the Psalmist has "sought your precepts," there is no worry of being distracted or detoured. However, when we seek God's precepts, we see that not all available paths are good.

Verse 46: When we have internalized the Words of God, when we have been trained by God's commandments we will be able to speak in the presence of kings and paupers and not be phased. The reality of what we learn from God is that it is good for anyone. Status is not a determining factor in who is worthy of hearing the testimonies of God.

Verse 47: The idea of "delight" is one easy to overlook. Whatever view of God's commands we have will affect how we understand that benefit to us. If we have a negative view of God's commands we will find little reason to delight in them. However, if we see them as a blessing, as a gift, as the way God conforms us into the image of Jesus, then we may see reasons to delight in them with greater ease and frequency.

Verse 48: In this verse we have two references. One to commandments and one to statutes. As we have seen already these are synonymous throughout the Psalm. It is interesting that with reference to God's commandment the Psalmist is reaching out for them. And the reason for this is they love God's commandments. Again, consider the previous verse's idea of delight because it should be kept in view. There is then a shift from affection to contemplation. The writer not only loves God's commandments but will meditate upon what God has established, which is what a statute infers. And so should we. We should love and meditate on what God has said continually.

Psalm 119:49-52

⁴⁹ Remember *your word* to your servant, in which you have made me hope.
⁵⁰ This is my comfort in my affliction, that *your promise* gives me life.
⁵¹ The insolent utterly deride me, but I do not turn away from *your law*.
⁵² When I think of *your rules* from of old, I take comfort, O Lord.

Reflection

When we find ourselves in dark places emotionally, the kind and compassionate words of a friend can bring relief. How much more the words of God when the darkness seems to deepen? Where do we turn when the enduring darkness of night does not seem to yield to the breaking of day?

Too often we surrender to the dark. Not because we want to. We surrender because we don't know what else to do. We are lost and without bearings to recalibrate our compass. This can be a difficult time for our souls.

As believers in God, as disciples of Christ, as travelers on the way, we have a different option. We have a better way. A way that cannot fail, even when we feel like victory is still a long way off.

The word of the Lord serves as light in dark times. As a balm when we find ourselves wounded and in pain. As a cool drink of water upon parched lips. As a river of joy for a sorrow-filled soul. The word of God is not like the good words of thoughtful men.

The word of God is the written revelation of the all-wise God. From God's lips to our ears; through our ears to our souls, the word of God can penetrate and mend what seemed utterly broken.

One of my fears is that we too often have too low a view of God's word. And because of this, we have too little confidence in God to perform what he has written. We have to hedge our bets and in doing so we have uprooted our faith from the only fertile soil in which it can flourish.

Commentary

Verse 49: The link between what God has promised to what we can have confidence in is unbreakable. It endures because God has forged the bond in the fire of his own character. The Psalmist reminds God of what he has promised. And it is within the context of this promise that the writer has placed their hope.

Verse 50: The Psalmist extends the idea of comfort here. They explicitly link together the comfort they feel in the midst of the "affliction" they may find themselves. An amplification of what the writer understands God's promise to be is provided. The promise made and guaranteed by God is that there is life attached to it. This serves as a sure foundation for our hope and peace.

Verse 51: Opposition to the faith of any and every believer should be expected. This means the world outside of the community of faith does not share the values or objectives of God's people. Therefore, their approval is not required for our obedience to God's commands. This further implies there is no legitimate reason to ever "turn away from your law."

Verse 52: This is the first time the Psalmist makes a reference to the "age" of God's rules. They say the rules come "from of old." These are not new rules. They were not the result of some recent or current event. To be more accurate they are as old as God himself. Which is to say, they are eternal rules, truths, commandments, precepts, etc. There is nothing new about what God is calling us to do. We can take comfort in this because it means we can trust God. God does not change, and he does not amend what he has required of us either.

Psalm 119:53-56

⁵³ Hot indignation seizes me because of
   the wicked, who forsake *your law*.
⁵⁴ *Your statutes* have been my songs in the
   house of my sojourning.
⁵⁵ I remember your name in the night,
   O Lord, and keep *your law*.
⁵⁶ This blessing has fallen to me, that I have
   kept *your precepts*.

Reflection

The longer we meditate on and linger with God's word, the greater our ability to understand God's heart. The word is not a window into the mysteries of God's being. Rather it is like water washing away what has been keeping us from seeing clearly.

The world can put so much in our way, it can become difficult to notice what God is doing. We have to continually wash all of that debris away. We have to diligently make the effort to keep our vision clear.

It can feel like a daunting task, but the fact we have God's word means we can do it. Maybe not perfectly.

Maybe even not like we would like to. But if we keep using the cleansing properties of God's word we will see with renewed eyes.

It can be difficult to make sense of how God's word works in our lives. It certainly can. The question is whether we will fight through those insecurities and persevere until the end.

Commentary

Verse 53: When we know God's word; when we have accepted the word's role in how we live and think; and then we see some who are blatantly living and speaking against what God has given, it can be anger inducing. But why? Because they forsake God's law and then seem to prosper. Or they forsake God's law and then rail against all we have seen and heard from God. This is one of the more candid confessions in the Psalm. Its presence is helpful, instructive, and liberating. It means we can be honest with God and God is not bothered by our struggles.

Verse 54: The idea of the words of God being like the Psalmist's "songs" in those places that are not home is an interesting perspective. The safety and security God's word affords his people is without equal. It is a wonder so few take advantage of what we have access to. Seeing God's statutes as something worthy of singing about may appear strange to us, but maybe that line of thought must be challenged and recalibrated.

Verse 55: Particularly in poetic language, when the word "night" is used, it usually means more than just the time of day. From a metaphorical standpoint it points to separation from God. However, within the context of Psalm 119, we see that night has a slightly different emphasis. Here, it appears to us, the Psalmist is using night to describe those times when it would be easy to dismiss or ignore or become lazy in holding onto God's law. This is why it is important to remember it. Because when we forget, we lose the light of our path in times and places where God is least felt as present.

Verse 56: In the keeping of God's precepts, there is a blessing already contained within our faithful obedience. We too often think our obedience will be the catalysts for some other blessing. What we must learn to appreciate is the fact that our living in obedience is evidence of God's gracious intervention in our lives. When we are living out what God has commanded, we can rejoice in how God has transformed our minds and hearts to the point we desire to obey. This in itself is a blessing.

Psalm 119:57-60

⁵⁷ The Lord is my portion; I promise to
  keep *your words*.
⁵⁸ I entreat your favor with all my heart;
  be gracious to me according
  to *your promise*.
⁵⁹ When I think on my ways, I turn my feet
  to *your testimonies*;
⁶⁰ I hasten and do not delay to
  keep *your commandments*.

Reflection

When our lives are dependent on who God is rather than on what God provides, we will find it easier to live in and through difficult circumstances. We are no longer slaves to the events of life, whether good or bad.

The reality of God's provision is too often tied to material things. While God can and has provided for people in physical ways, the deeper promise is to give us himself. To open the doors of his throne room and allow us in. This is the true treasure of a relationship with God.

To be a child of God is to have access to the only one who can free us from the trials and tribulations of this broken world. This is why we must rely upon God's word as a guide and teacher. It prepares us for and positions us in the right mindset to live with God.

Commentary

Verse 57: The link between God's sustaining power and our faithful obedience should not be overlooked. When we live in accord to God's commands we become the beneficiaries of God's very person. This is one of the reasons we are instructed by Jesus to pray for "daily bread." We are to depend upon God first. If he provides for us through supernatural means (like manna from the sky) or through natural means (like a good job) we are to give God thanks for his presence.

Verse 58: One of the many comforts of a relationship with God is how we are able to approach God. We are not cut off from God. We are able to approach God and to be heard by him. This is comforting because it means God's discipline will not be punitive. It will not destroy us. When we know God's love, we can have peace of mind regarding how God will deal with us when we have faltered in our daily living.

Verse 59: Self-reflection is an important and underutilized practice. We do not have to take a negative view of ourselves to know we still have a lot to learn. Having this awareness is a powerful reminder of how much we need God's word. The more time we spend in it, the clearer our understanding of what we need to address in our lives. Perfection is not the goal of the journey of faith. Maturity is the goal. And this, to put it plainly, means living according to who God is and who we are in Christ.

Verse 60: Diligence is a word that should define our interaction with God's word. We should not just know the contents of Scripture. We should be striving to align our thoughts and actions to what they teach. The connection between knowledge and practice should be strengthened as we grow on this journey toward God.

Psalm 119:61-64

⁶¹ Though the cords of the wicked ensnare
  me, I do not forget *your law*.
⁶² At midnight I rise to praise you, because
  of *your righteous rules*.
⁶³ I am a companion of all who fear you, of
  those who keep *your precepts*.
⁶⁴ The earth, O Lord, is full of your
  steadfast love; teach me *your statutes*!

Reflection

The company we keep will influence two important aspects of life. Our friends will impact our perspective on life and our ability to overcome challenges.

How we view the world is greatly informed by the people we have around us. If they generally have a negative view of the world and of how events will turn out, we will find ourselves mimicking that as well. However, if they are positive and look for the "win," that will also inform, to varying degrees, how we approach the circumstances of life we encounter.

The second area our friends impact us has to do with our resilience. Now, this does not mean that you don't ever get down or discombobulated. It just means, based on the description above, if our friends have a dim view, it is easier to stay out of sorts. The inverse is also being true. Upbeat and positive friends look for ways to pick you up. Even if we are not quick to change our attitude or thinking, it can be helpful to know there are others there to support you.

These are not hard and fast rules. They are broad descriptions being borne out in my life. But it should be clear, we are not talking about a naive view of the world. We are talking about recognizing how who we associate with has a greater effect on us than we may like to admit.

Commentary

Verse 61: In the course of living, there are times where others may want to cause us harm. And regardless of the way that harm comes, it can create in us anxiety and worry about our lives. These kinds of situations cannot all be avoided. So, we must make every effort to be prepared. In the verse we see how preparation is best achieved, from the perspective of faith, when we do not "forget your law." In God's commandments, we find wisdom for how to overcome and even endure difficult seasons.

Verse 62: As we mentioned briefly in another section, descriptions of the time of day are many times metaphorical. Referring to some other contextual idea. In this case, it would appear that the reference to "midnight" is another reference to difficulty or times when our peace is being challenged. In these times we ought to still find reasons to praise God. And our praise will make more sense because we are grounded in God's revelation. In those words, preserved for us in the Scripture, we make discoveries of God's goodness and his manifold promises. These discoveries open up for us newer and deeper and better insights of who God truly is.

Verse 63: Walking by faith can feel daunting at times. However, there is great comfort in knowing we do not walk alone. The Psalmist acknowledges that there are others who also fear the Lord. And it is those fellow travelers who make up the body of the faithful. Our shared faith works to strengthen us and encourage us throughout our journey. What should not be overlooked is that the writer is talking about a specific group of people. Not just anyone meets the criteria for this cohort. It is those who "keep your precepts" who are to be seen as fellow journeymen.

Verse 64: God's love is the attribute of his character most clearly seen in Jesus. The work of redemption on and through the cross are key to understanding God's love toward us. What is remarkable here is the description of where God's love resides. It exists and is seen in the whole earth. The creation is a testament to God's love for us. When we recognize this, we can "see" more of God's love. The connection to God's word is this, as we see God's love in creation (or what is often called "general revelation") we can then see God's love in his Word (or "special revelation"). God is at work in the natural world, and he is at work in the spiritual world. It is not one or the other, it is both. And usually at the same time.

Psalm 119:65-68

⁶⁵ You have dealt well with your servant,
   O Lord, according to *your word*.
⁶⁶ Teach me good judgment
   and knowledge, for I believe
   in *your commandments*.
⁶⁷ Before I was afflicted I went astray,
   but now I keep *your word*.
⁶⁸ You are good and do good;
   teach me *your statutes*.

Reflection

The word of God has a purpose we often miss. And the reason we miss it is we have made an incorrect assumption for why God provided a written testament of his will. The purpose we miss is that God wants to shape our characters by the words he has given to us. To reduce the word of God to a book of regulations and restrictions is to miss the redeemed understanding Jesus's life and ministry sought to establish. When we begin to look at the word of God as the instrument God uses to conform our thoughts and wills to his heart, we may very well begin to see the growth we long for.

The underlying assumption for why we miss this purpose is much simpler than we may want to concede. We don't want anyone telling us what to do! We don't mind if God tells us what he doesn't like. But anything more than that and we chafe at the thought of it.

We think that heeding God's word and obeying God's commands will amount to a repressive restriction upon our person. The problem with thinking this way is it says a great deal about what we believe about God's intentions toward us. God is "good and [does] good."

To fail to trust in God's eternal goodness is to reject everything else we think we know about God. The more we fight against God's goodness the more difficult we make our ability to grow. If God restricts our access to something, we should rejoice. It means God has our best interests at heart. He knows more than we will ever understand. To trust God, even when we do not fully understand, is the best decision we can ever make.

Commentary

Verse 65: God will deal with all of us according to the same standard, his word. What this means is God does not show any favoritism toward any one person. The commonly used word in the scriptures to describe this is "impartiality." God applies the same standard to all people. That is comforting. It means we are no better or no worse off before God. God will deal with us without comparing us to anyone else.

Verse 66: Having "good judgment and knowledge" should be something every believer seeks. But, how are we to acquire it? How do we maximize our chances of attaining these good qualities? Interestingly, the writer of Psalm 119 says they come through our believing in God's commandments. What makes this an odd relationship is we are often told to understand so that we can believe. However, what if, in God's economy of things, when we believe we come to know? While we may intuitively seek to know first, it may well be worth our energy to believe first and see how that improves our knowing.

Verse 67: We have to recognize the connection between our disobedience to God's word and our going astray. If we don't we will wonder why our choices never seem to satisfy our longing. Going astray from God is the preceding action to being afflicted. We are not afflicted because we go astray. When we go astray from God is when affliction can come. And if we are afflicted when we are away from God, we don't have God to lean on. When we keep God's word, we are setting ourselves up to be comforted by God because we know what God expects of and desires for us.

Verse 68: The testimony of the Psalmist is that God is both good and a doer of good. This description of God is helpful because it reminds us that God's character does not change. We can expect God to do good because of who he is. He is a good God. It is in the context of this goodness that we can call upon God to teach us his statutes. If we desire to be good like God, then we must learn to think and live like God as well.

Psalm 119:69-72

⁶⁹ The insolent smear me with lies,
    but with my whole heart I
    keep *your precepts*;
⁷⁰ their heart is unfeeling like fat, but I
    delight in *your law*.
⁷¹ It is good for me that I was afflicted, that
    I might learn *your statutes*.
⁷² *The law of your mouth* is better to me than
    thousands of gold and silver pieces.

Reflection

As the years have passed, the more wonderful and precious God's word becomes. The riches of its wisdom and the glory it conveys are unsurpassed.

There may have been a time when I thought I could live without the Scripture's influence in my life. I had treated the word as helpful advice, ancient wisdom, or just practical ideas for living. However, this is not what God's word is. It should not be reduced in this way.

God's laws, commandments, precepts, and statutes, all of these ways of seeing God's revelation, are

God's self-expression. God speaks into the world and we should take that effort more seriously than we do. We should give his utterances the proper weight they deserve, for they are the verbalization of God's mind.

So, when we read and meditate on God's word, we are interacting with the very mind of God. Let's therefore approach this priceless treasure with the dignity and care it merits.

Commentary

Verse 69: It does not matter what those who oppose us say or do, we must remain faithful to God's precepts. An important caveat here is this: we must not be guilty of what those who speak against us are saying. If we are being falsely maligned, we must not succumb to responding in kind. We must become more committed to living in accord with God's character. If we do not keep God precepts "with my whole heart," we give opportunities for our enemies, whether spiritual or physical, to find an entry point. We must work to fortify our defenses when under attack, to stand firm when the enemies push their advance.

Verse 70: As a continuation of the previous verse, the idea of "their heart" being incapable of feeling is quite interesting. It seems the reason for the smears is due to our attackers lack of "delight" in God's law. When we know God's law, and are being shaped by it, we refrain from doing to others what we do not want done to us. We are able to make links between actions and consequences. The law of God is the forge in which our conscience is molded. Without God's law, we become untethered to what is true and righteous. And once this has happened, we will indulge all manner of actions and activities that besmirch the name of God.

Verse 71: When given the choice between comfort and tribulation, it would be safe to say, most people would choose comfort. So, the idea here is not an invitation to tribulation, but a reframing of it. To be able to look at the difficult circumstances of life and to then see how God's word becomes real to us in those moments is an important component of a mature faith. The greater our focus on God's statutes, the better our ability to endure, even in the most difficult of times.

Verse 72: There is nothing that compares to the value of God's law. Not even gold and silver can be traded or exchanged for it. This view of the worth of God's law is one many overlook. In order to better understand what treasure we possess, we have to reconnect the object with the giver. When we see that God has given us this precious gift, we can better appreciate the importance of what we have been granted access to in the Scriptures.

Psalm 119:73-76

⁷³ Your hands have made and fashioned
    me; give me understanding that I may
    learn *your commandments*.
⁷⁴ Those who fear you shall see me
    and rejoice, because I have hoped
    in *your word*.
⁷⁵ I know, O Lord, that *your rules* are
    righteous, and that in faithfulness
    you have afflicted me.
⁷⁶ Let your steadfast love comfort
    me according to *your promise*
    to your servant.

Reflection

How do we know that God is at work in us? This is one of the most often asked questions by believers. And yet it is one of the most difficult questions to answer. Not because we cannot know, but because God works at a pace we don't always recognize.

There are times when God can, has, and does act with immediate effect. But the reality of God's activity in our lives is more often slow and steady. Nearly imperceptible to our natural eye and mind. It is a process that may even be described as unnoticeable. The reasons for this are two-fold. First, God is good and gracious. God knows what we can handle. So, he works in such a way that we are moving in a heavenward direction, but not so fast as to cause us to become discouraged or feel left behind.

The second reason for God's pacing is he knows if we see too much change too fast, we will become dependent on his provision rather than find comfort in his presence. The abiding presence of God is the true inheritance of his children. Everything else is an added bonus to this.

The word of God provides us the information we need for transformation. But that information takes time to work because we struggle to live in obedience to what we know it requires of us. And it is this obedience, or its absence, that helps us gauge how much fruit God has borne in us.

Commentary

Verse 73: We have been fashioned in the image of God. While the natural means of conception appear to keep us distant from God's personal act of creation, the reality is greater than we may understand. Every person conceived has imprinted within them that aspect of God's person that makes us unique and special. We are living monuments to God's glorious beauty. And when we recognize how his image becomes our visage, we will recognize why conforming our lives to his commands is so vital. When we live according to what God has said, we reflect him most clearly.

Verse 74: When we live in faithful submission to God's word, our hope becomes the joy of others who claim to belong to God as well. The bonds of confraternity that exist among those who share a common trust in God's word are powerful. But only when we embrace them as being so. To be known by those who know God's word is a great hope when times of difficulty arise.

Verse 75: A key realization for those who trust in God is to see his rules as good and helpful to us. They are not merely the restrictive impositions of a hard-hearted God. That is why when we are confronted with trials we can stand. We trust God to bring us through what comes our way. We may prefer to avoid the tribulations of life, but God most often delivers through and not just from what we find ourselves enduring in life.

Verse 76: What God has promised, God will fulfill. He has said that we will never be left alone nor forsaken. This is a powerful reminder of what we have when we are in fellowship with God. In a way, the Psalmist is demonstrating we have to allow ourselves to be loved by God. God already loves us, but we can behave in such a way that we do not feel it, even when it is present.

Psalm 119:77-80

⁷⁷ Let your mercy come to me, that I may live; for *your law* is my delight.
⁷⁸ Let the insolent be put to shame, because they have wronged me with falsehood; as for me, I will meditate on *your precepts*.
⁷⁹ Let those who fear you turn to me, that they may know *your testimonies*.
⁸⁰ May my heart be blameless in *your statutes*, that I may not be put to shame!

Reflection

It is quite remarkable how little we understand regarding the relationship between the word of God and the acts of men.

It is my theory that the reasons we know so little is because we have not stopped looking through the lenses of our denominations, our heroes in the faith, our favorite authors, etc., but that when we look at these things we are not also looking at Jesus.

Anything that moves us away from God, no matter how flattering the presentation cannot be trusted without some verification. And when we are thinking and talking with our neighbors, we must keep in mind that not everything said or heard needs to be repeated as gospel truth. It may not in fact be true.

But when it comes to God, God does not need to impress anyone. He is impressiveness personified. When God speaks, he speaks with all the authority befitting his place in the cosmos as God. And because of this we have to learn to see who God is in His person. Not just looking forward to what he can do for us. But to focus on who he is and be satisfied with that.

Commentary

Verse 77: When the word of God is our delight, we find it easier to see God's mercy. This may be one of the primary reasons we struggle to see and know God's mercy. God's word is what points to and describes what it means to experience God's mercy. With the world the idea of mercy is often superficial and fluid. But when God speaks of mercy, we can trust it will mean the same thing to all who find need of it.

Verse 78: When those who oppose God's will and ways cross our path, we may be surprised at their distaste for followers of God. We may not want to think like this. Or even to consider this state of affairs is possible. But Jesus said that since the world had no need of him, it would have no need for us. But regardless of what the world does, we have to meditate and deeply consider what God's word points to. To become distracted is to short circuit what God is working in us.

Verse 79: This verse has an underlying evangelistic implication. The idea of having those who seek after God to turn to the Psalmist is odd from an Old Testament perspective. But when we realize that God has always called his people to share his goodness to the world we see the idea differently. The reason for requesting this kind of relationship is so that the writer can tell of what God has done. It can often be overlooked, and even dismissed, but one of the best things any congregant can hear every week is God's word. Without it we are lost and without it we have no reason to share the gospel with those who are lost and separated from God living around us.

Verse 80: Throughout the psalm, we catch glimpses of the author's struggles. The struggle to live in accord with God's expectation can be daunting. But if we stick to what God has revealed, we may discover how much easier it is to live before God. Holiness is a difficult topic, and yet we are called to cultivate a life in keeping with this ideal. Being blameless is not that you never make a mistake. It's a commitment to continue to grow toward God, in spite of the inadequacies we see in the mirror.

Psalm 119:81-84

⁸¹ My soul longs for your salvation;
    I hope in *your word*.
⁸² My eyes long for *your promise*; I ask,
    "When will you comfort me?"
⁸³ For I have become like a wineskin in
    the smoke, yet I have not forgotten
    your statutes.
⁸⁴ How long must your servant endure?
    When will you judge those who
    persecute me?

Reflection

The language of "longing" has been mostly lost in the modern world. We speak more of desire and wanting. But these words tend to be used to capture ideas of seeking immediate relief or fulfillment. If we can just get what we want, we will be better. Even better off. The truth, however, is that is not how things happen.

But longing, and in particular, the biblical conceptualization of it, speaks to an all-encompassing satisfaction that will not be met by just anything.

Especially not anything in this world. The longing the Psalmist is speaking to is an awareness that what is missing in our lives is of a spiritual nature. That the void that must be filled is as vast as God is eternal.

Only God can satisfy what is missing in us because it is God who created us to exist with him. The separation we commonly call sin, in theological terms, is the emptiness created by the distance our disobedience creates. The greater the distance the more ravenous the longing. And the longer we exist in this condition, the more desperate we feel. This is why when we try to fill the emptiness, we feel with the options the world provides, it only deepens the despair within and thickens the darkness around us.

But the closer we draw to God, the more satisfied we become. The lighter our burdens get, the clearer our path before us. We will find ourselves not looking for something to fill that space where we know something is missing. Rather, we can then begin to look to God and be fulfilled as we were always meant to be.

Commentary

Verse 81: To know God's word is to know the hope God offers. To believe what God has revealed is to see what God can and has done. As these realities and realizations take root within our minds and hearts a longing for God's promised blessings take root. In particular, we begin to see salvation as God's greatest gift. The one from which all others emanate. And the one we should seek above all others.

Verse 82: On our journey of faith, the more time we spend with God, the more accustomed we become to his presence. This does not mean we will not have times of drift. We are a people who must always fight for a disciplined way of living. However, our proximity to God is a constant reminder of the joy of his promises. When we have tasted and seen, it becomes more difficult to ignore what we are missing out on in our distance from God.

Verse 83: The imagery here is of a wineskin no longer in use, set aside, and allowed to fall into disrepair because of smoke, usually in the place of a tent where food was cooked and prepared. With this picture in mind, we are to see the effect of being dismissed or ostracized unjustly. To be kept from fulfilling one's purpose. In spite of these circumstances, we are encouraged to not forget what God has commanded. God's purposes for us are not at risk, just because we find ourselves in places not of our design.

Verse 84: This is the first verse in which the Psalmist does not make some direct reference or allusion to God's word. Over and over again, the author was pointing back to how all God had spoken had impacted and guided their life. After reflecting and considering all the good that comes through obedience to God's commands, there is a pause and a question for God. How long must there be suffering for continued faithfulness to what God has said? At this point, there is no answer. Only the question.

And the wrestling that comes from seeking God in the midst of difficulties brought about by injustice.

Psalm 119:85-88

⁸⁵ The insolent have dug pitfalls for me;
   they do not live according to *your law*.
⁸⁶ All *your commandments* are sure; they
   persecute me with falsehood; help me!
⁸⁷ They have almost made an end of
   me on earth, but I have not forsaken
   your precepts.
⁸⁸ In your steadfast love give me life, that I
   may keep *the testimonies of your mouth*.

Reflection

The Psalmist offers an interesting perspective about what should be most valued in life. In the final verse of this section, the writer makes a request for continued life. That the life to be given is the consequence or result of God's steadfast love.

What is interesting, and even verges on the peculiar, is the reason for the request for life. The Psalmist desires to live so that they may keep, or observe, the testimonies of God. What God had said was worthy of continuing to live so as to enjoy God's testimonies even longer.

It is an odd time to walk on the earth. There are so many who value the word of God so little. They crack open its pages when there is sufficient time, or just when it is convenient. This is a sad and unhealthy way of interacting with God and his word. We should see God's word as a treasure worth treasuring. But the circumstances of life can keep our focus away from this wonderful gift we have been given and is at our fingertips.

Our keeping of God's word is not the means of attracting God's attention. We must remove this from our minds. Our observance and obedience to God's word is the result of our having received God's incalculable love. As we experience God's grace we are awakened to the wonder and majesty of God's word.

Until we see this relationship clearly, we will interact with God in transactional ways, rather than spiritual and relationship ways. We will attempt to bribe or manipulate God. And even though it is not possible, we will expect God to act in ways inconsistent with his character.

Commentary

Verse 85: When people choose to reject the law of God as a standard for living, they become susceptible to all manner of unethical acts. But they also become potential perpetrators of those same kinds of behaviors. To live in conformity to God's prescription is to create a spiritual and moral division between us and the world. Not with the intention of creating obstacles for others, but as a consequence of our faithfulness being a reminder of their lack of it. Living in obedience and conformity to God's law will highlight the differences between us. We should neither be surprised or dismayed by this.

This is one of the many challenges of the Christian journey. We are to live in the light of God's holiness, but that very activity causes those outside of that relationship to resent us for it. We become constant reminders of God. And for some, that is not a reality they desire to entertain. Therefore, we are forced to choose between the approval of God over that of men.

Verse 86: The surety, or the constancy, of God's commandments are a comfort in times of persecution. To know that God will never go back on his word can be a boon in times of great difficulty. What is also important to note is the nature of the persecution. It comes because "falsehoods" had to be told to conjure up the negative pressure against the child of God. If those of the world are to make our lives difficult, let it be because they had to fabricate the reasons. It can be encouraging, in spite of the pain, that what they are saying about us are lies and what they are doing to us is unjust.

Verse 87: Continuing on the theme of having those in the world coming against us, we see how important God's word is to the Psalmist. The burden of the attacks were so severe, they had brought them to the point of death. The implication is that the writer was as close as they had ever been to perishing. And yet, in the midst of the upheaval, the thought of forsaking God's precepts was dismissed. No level of discomfort and no degree of danger should dislodge our commitment to God's precepts. It will take courage to live in this way.

Verse 88: The love of God is described as being steadfast. The immovable reality of God's love is a key to our holding onto our faith. It means we can trust God. With this reality in view, the Psalmist calls upon God to give them life. After all that had come against them in the previous verses, it is no wonder we see this request. However, the reason for the continued sustaining of life was not just personal entertainment or pleasure. The purpose of the Psalmist's life was to be able to keep the testimonies of God. In linking continued life with the keeping of God's testimonies, what we find is one of the deepest and most important reasons we can endure the attacks we face in our lives. What God has said, God will do. And what God has promised, nothing can deter.

Psalm 119:89-92

⁸⁹ Forever, O Lord, *your word* is firmly fixed in the heavens.
⁹⁰ Your faithfulness endures to all generations; you have established the earth, and it stands fast.
⁹¹ By your appointment they stand this day, for all things are your servants.
⁹² If *your law* had not been my delight, I would have perished in my affliction.

Reflection

There is one aspect of God's character that may be, at least to me, the most comforting. We see it here described as God's faithfulness.

When I think about one of my great concerns in the Christian journey, it is wondering if God's attitude toward me will ever change. Will my struggles and weakness become too much for God to tolerate? Will we fail one too many times? And what is more horrifying, will I even know if that moment comes?

But, when we see verses like this, I find great comfort. God is faithful, but his faithfulness is not limited to my time or culture. God's ability to remain true to his word and consistent to his character are realities that transcend one generation. What God offered and promised to Moses is still true for us. Not because we are wiser than Moses, but because God is just as good to us as he was to him.

God is faithful. And for that I am grateful.

Commentary

Verse 89: God's word is unchanging. The fixed nature of what God has spoken is a guarantee of God's promises. God will never reject or countermand his word. This reality is what we build our faith on. There has never been a time when God has vacillated in keeping his word. This fortitude is what gives us confidence in believing today what God has said in the past. But it also fosters hope that we can expect in the future what God has promised to us today.

Verse 90: God's faithfulness is one of the great mysteries of the Christian journey. We all know we are frail and inconsistent. We all, at some point in our lives, struggle to do what we know God expects of us. It is one of the great sources of discouragement. To know what we should do, and still be unable to perform it in our daily journey. But God's goodness and kindness toward us is most gloriously seen when God continues to give us what we do not deserve, his grace.

Verse 91: All God has created persists because of God's sustaining power. Nothing exists apart from God's presence. He not only created, but he maintains the parameters of existence itself. Without God nothing can exist. But with God, even that which rejects him, cannot escape his influence. God may not impose, but nothing can prevent him from being where he chooses to be.

Verse 92: We find here another reference to delighting in God's law. This is a theme for which we, in our modern times, have few points of reference. We struggle to see how the Law of God and the grace of God exist in a harmonious relationship. Discovering this connection is key to experiencing what the Psalmist describes here. To delight in God's law provides for us a ballast of hope and relief in times of great struggle. When these times of affliction come, if we have waited to delight in God's law, we will have waited too long.

Psalm 119:93-96

⁹³ I will never forget *your precepts,* for by
  them you have given me life.
⁹⁴ I am yours; save me, for I have
  sought *your precepts.*
⁹⁵ The wicked lie in wait to destroy me,
  but I consider *your testimonies.*
⁹⁶ I have seen a limit to all perfection,
  but *your commandment* is
  exceedingly broad.

Reflection

When we become children of God, a transfer of "ownership" has taken place. It may be better to say that a transfer of responsibility has taken place.

The day I learned I would become a father, I felt a weight settle on me. In that moment, there was a realization that I would become responsible for a new life. To say I was changed by that awakening would be an understatement. I was shaken by the changes I knew would become a part of my life.

In many ways, I knew I would never be the same again. I understand how I saw the world would be altered by the presence of this new life in my home.

While it would be a little foolish to try and describe what God feels for us as his children, I do think we can learn something from the Psalmist's description in verse 94. We no longer belong to ourselves. When we have entered into a relationship with God by faith in Jesus, we have surrendered our rights to our own lives.

There may be some who are bothered by this. I am not one of them. To know God is responsible for my life, my soul, and my destiny is quite comforting. I don't always appreciate it like I should. So, it would be wise to do what I can to not lose sight of this wonderful reality.

Commentary

Verse 93: Here we see an explicit connection being made between God's precepts and the life we have. The idea of "life" here can be understood in a variety of ways. It could be salvation. Or it could mean encouragement. However, the overall tone of the psalm leans in a practical direction. Therefore, with that in mind, it would make sense to see the word "life" here as referring to wisdom. As we learn and remember God's word, we grow in wisdom. We are enlightened by the mind of God for how we should conduct ourselves in this world.

Verse 94: The pursuit of God's precepts is an indication of what we value. The greater our commitment to God's word, the more we understand all God has promised. The way we see our relationship with God also has a role to play here. The Psalmist describes themselves as belonging to God, "I am yours." This is the posture of the person who sees all God offers and chooses that over anything else.

Verse 95: The fact of opposition should be a given in the believer's life. It will happen in the course of time. Not always because of something we did to instigate it. Sometimes we are faced with conflict because we are doing what God has commanded. In this verse the Psalmist implies that regardless of what may come against us, we should "consider your testimonies." We should cultivate a resolve to not lose sight of what God has revealed to us. This consideration is a safeguard against losing heart in the midst of the schemes of the wicked.

Verse 96: The expanse of God's commandments cannot be measured and it cannot be quantified. In the world, there are those who would try and convince us of their wisdom. But earthly wisdom has its limits. What's more, earthly wisdom can never bring us into the presence of God. God's commands may at first appear restrictive, but they are far greater than we may fully understand in the moment. They lead us to a more vibrant freedom than we could imagine on our own. So, as we dive deeper and investigate further and consider more intentionally what God has commanded, we will see the richness of God's wisdom like never before.

Psalm 119:97-100

⁹⁷ Oh how I love *your law*! It is my
 meditation all the day.
⁹⁸ *Your commandment* makes me wiser than
 my enemies, for it is ever with me.
⁹⁹ I have more understanding than
 all my teachers, for *your testimonies*
 are my meditation.
¹⁰⁰ I understand more than the aged,
 for I keep *your precepts*.

Reflection

There is one thing in life that we should all be diligent in cultivating. That "thing" is wisdom. Wisdom is the greatest weapon against living a life of confusion and wandering. When we are wise, even when we cannot avoid hard situations, we can have a perspective that leads us through the hardships.

As a follower of Christ, we have been given access to the greatest treasure trove of wisdom imaginable. It is called the Bible. The richness of this treasure is in the fact it is not the wisdom of other human beings. It is the very wisdom of God.

God has revealed himself in and through the normal, everyday events of the human experience. This means the Bible contains two important attributes. First, the word of God has a plethora of points of contact that make sense to us because they are, oftentimes, typical human events. We can learn to see ourselves in the moments that are captured within the texts.

Second, and this one is very exciting to me, the wisdom of God is knowable because God wanted us to learn how to live. When we see God working through the foibles and weaknesses of other human beings, we can be confident that the lessons can be transferred to those who would listen. But we have to be listening. We have to take notice of how we can get caught up in the same kinds of circumstances. This ability to connect the dots is vital to our growing in wisdom.

Commentary

Verse 97: Given the fact that the longest Psalm in the Bible is about the Word of God, it should be no surprise that the Psalmist speaks glowingly of God's law. "Oh how I love your law!" This ought to be the attitude of those who have spent time with what God has said. This is the way those who have been impacted and changed by what God has declared should feel. However, we cannot love what we do not understand. We will not meditate on it "all the day" when we have an indifferent or even a negative view of God's word.

Verse 98: The search for wisdom is a perpetual one. What we must recognize is that the finding of wisdom requires humility. There is a need for acceptance of what we have and what we are missing. There is no sense in which we can claim "we have arrived." What is interesting here is that when we embrace God's commandments, we become wiser than our enemies. What this means is we do not have to worry about what they are doing. Their efforts will come to nothing. Our continual trust in God's commandments gives us comfort and strength when confronted by those who seek to do us harm.

Verse 99: In this verse, the Psalmist continues this theme of wisdom. Here it is called "understanding." There is a trap we all are susceptible to if we are not careful. It is called "appealing to authority." This is the viewpoint that we should defer to those in positions of authority. They may be in those positions because they know something we don't. And while experience and training are definitely considerations when evaluating someone's credibility, there is one significant problem. No one, no matter who they are or what they claim to know, can claim to be the ultimate authority on a topic. No one, except God. And to know God is to know the one who knows all. That is why knowing what God knows is better than knowing what human experts claim to know. Even if what they know is true.

Verse 100: In this section we see the movement from having more wisdom than enemies, then to more than teachers, and now more than "the aged." Living a long life has a way of teaching us many lessons. But even a lifetime of experience cannot be compared to the wisdom that comes from obedience to God's precepts. There is a mystery in the Psalmist's structure here. In order to understand it, we have to accept the key being offered to us. The key to the kind of wisdom being described is a sincere trust and commitment to God's word. It is as easy and as hard as that.

Psalm 119:101-104

¹⁰¹ I hold back my feet from every evil way,
    in order to keep *your word*.
¹⁰² I do not turn aside from *your rules*, for
    you have taught me.
¹⁰³ How sweet are *your words* to my taste,
    sweeter than honey to my mouth!
¹⁰⁴ Through *your precepts* I get
    understanding; therefore
    I hate every false way.

Reflection

The longer we spend time with God's word, the easier it becomes to tell the difference between right and wrong. The reason is quite simple. Simpler than we may be ready to admit. It becomes easier because we now have access to how God sees the world, including how he sees us.

When our thoughts are transformed by the word of God and our lives are conformed to the example of Christ, we begin to understand what would please God. In the same way that familiarity can make us more keenly aware of the preferences of our loved ones, when we know what God commands and what God desires, we develop an awareness of what is congruent with God's character.

Pleasing God is not complicated. But it does take a commitment to living in the light of his word. Pleasing God requires us to set aside trying to please those around us. As we learn what the Scriptures teach, and as we grow in our ability to recognize those things that are in line with it, we can actually respond more consistently to the variety of circumstances we may encounter.

The easiest way I have come to explain what this means is this: We have to make decisions based on what God says, not what we feel. Our feelings will try and convince us that what is now before us matters more than the eternal truth of God. The proximity of the issue will confuse us if we are not grounded in who God is. God does not change. Therefore, whatever we do must not make it appear that God has changed.

Commentary

Verse 101: There is a link between our obedience to God's word and the choices we make in life. It will be very rare the number of times where we will know what the consequences of our decisions will be. There are so many variables in life. This is why it is both wise and prudent to make choices that lead us toward greater submission to God. What this means is as we learn what God has commanded, we do those things to the best of our ability.

The greater our consistency, the lower the likelihood we will choose paths that are evil or lead to evil.

Verse 102: In a variety of instances, we have seen the Psalmist thank God for his instruction. This is the clearest instance of that sentiment. When we know who the teacher is, our confidence grows in what we are taught. So, what are we to think when our teacher is God? We should disregard what God says less and less.

Verse 103: The image of eating God's word and of the sweet taste it has is a vivid one. The Psalmist is adamant in their conviction that God's words are the best things in the world. There is nothing better than having and consuming and savoring the wisdom of God in the Scriptures. In order to understand this, we have to take the full weight of what we have seen up to this point in the psalm into account. The blessings and benefits of obedience to God's word cannot be calculated, but they can be experienced.

Verse 104: This verse recalls what was said in v. 101. While there might be some relative difference between the "evil" path and the "wrong" path, the difference in effect may not be as different at all. To choose or go down any path that leads away from God's purposes will invariably reveal a failure to obey God's word.

Psalm 119:105-108

¹⁰⁵ *Your word* is a lamp to my feet and a
  light to my path.
¹⁰⁶ I have sworn an oath and confirmed it,
  to keep *your righteous rules.*
¹⁰⁷ I am severely afflicted; give me life, O
  Lord, according to *your word!*
¹⁰⁸ Accept my freewill offerings of praise, O
  Lord, and teach me *your rules.*

Reflection

There are many different kinds of challenges on this journey of faith. The variety stems from the uniqueness of each person. No two people, even if they experienced the identical events, would be affected in the same way. Each person is as different as the proverbial snowflakes.

Understanding how wide the possible responses could be helps us to better appreciate the beauty of God's word. As we approach the Scriptures, each and every person who embraces them will be ministered to in just the ways they need. This characteristic of the Bible can only be described as miraculous.

How does knowing this help us? I believe it gives us a confidence in God's ability to lead us where we may not go otherwise. If we know that when we read and meditate and internalize God's wisdom he is present with us, this increases our desire to drink of that well over and over again.

To trust the Bible is not merely a blind assent. It is a tested decision. But if we have not actually conformed our thoughts to the patterns it teaches we may never actually know. Too often in my own life I have claimed my own wisdom and understanding for God's. This is always a mistake. And it is always a fool's errand. It is not until we truly submit to God's word that we will see the harvest of God's word bear fruit in our lives.

Commentary

Verse 105: This may possibly be one of the best known verses of Psalm 119. The two-fold blessing of God's word is it helps us to see where we are AND where we are going. Being able to have a stable footing is vitally important to living confidently before God. Also, knowing we are headed in the correct direction builds our trust in God's goodness. We see here God accomplishes all this through his word.

Verse 106: It takes a conscious decision to keep God's rules. It is not something we just fall into doing. The principal reason is we really do not want to. The Psalmist says they have confirmed their oath. One has to wonder how this confirmation has taken place. The simplest way of thinking about it is to remember the context of Psalm 119 up to this point. The context is a trust in God's word to provide all that has been described. This steady trust is a perpetual confirmation. Both to God, but also to us. As we do what we have promised, God does what he has promised. And with each step, faith is built up in us.

Verse 107: At first glance it would be easy to describe the Psalmist's plea as a request for protection. This would not be an incorrect reading. However, there is another, more subtle implication of the text. Namely, that the word of God described a particular understanding of what life is. The life of faith cannot be quantified in the same terms as that of a life without God. This would be to impose upon God that which he is under no obligation to provide.

Verse 108: Thankfulness and worship are always appropriate responses to God's goodness. Especially when we offer them for no other reason than to let God know we are thankful. As we appreciate God's grace and mercy we ought to make it a habit to honor God without needing to be prompted. As we give thanks to God, we are also preparing ourselves to receive instruction from him.

Psalm 119:109-112

¹⁰⁹ I hold my life in my hand continually,
   but I do not forget *your law*.
¹¹⁰ The wicked have laid a snare for me, but
   I do not stray from *your precepts*.
¹¹¹ *Your testimonies* are my heritage forever,
   for they are the joy of my heart.
¹¹² I incline my heart to perform *your
   statutes* forever, to the end.

Reflection

What do we do when we cannot seem to find the answer we need in God's word? We can get frustrated or discouraged. When this happens, we consider abandoning the scriptures in search of an alternate source of wisdom. This is a terrible mistake. One we are all capable of making. And may have already made.

Over the course of the last twenty years, I have learned that an important part of my anxiety over God's silence is me. I come to God believing God is obligated to bend to my every whim. This is not only wrong, but it also exposes an assumption that hinders our relationship with God. When we demand God act, we have usurped an authority that does not belong to us. God does not answer to me.

The Psalmist throughout this psalm provides us with a multitude of reasons why we should never demand of God what God has not obligated himself to do in his word. The Word of God is a binding document, both to God and to us. In it we find everything we need to know about how God operates in the world and how we are to approach him.

God will not do anything contrary to what he has revealed. And if we approach God understanding who he is and how he works, we reduce (and maybe even eliminate) the reasons for our frustration.

Commentary

Verse 109: Every day we make important decisions that will affect the course of our lives. These decisions do not always feel significant, but which ones will or will not be cannot be predicted. To live with our eyes set on eternity is the best way of honoring the gift of life we have. So, it is vital that one of those decisions we make is to remember God's law. To acknowledge that what God has commanded also requires our attention every day.

Verse 110: This theme of the plans of those who are against us has been repeated several times. And each time the general direction is that of distraction. When there are people working to harm us, it can draw our attention from what we should be doing. Whether that is an objective or one of God's "precepts." The Psalmist admits the reality of this opposition and at the same time encourages us to recognize that a commitment to what God has said is far better.

Verse 111: As children of God, God's word is an inheritance to us. The beauty of this inheritance is we do not have to wait to enjoy it. We have access to it right now. All we have to do is make ourselves available to it. When we love the giver, we will treasure the gift even more. This is why we must read and meditate and study the Bible. It is ours by right. To not enjoy it is to diminish the one who provided it for us.

Verse 112: There comes a moment on our journey of faith when we understand what is required of us. When that moment comes, we must make a choice. There is no way of not making a choice. We will either choose to obey or to disobey. This same moment will occur when we understand what the word of God is to us. At that moment we will have to make a choice. Will we do all God has commanded? Or will we make a different choice?

Psalm 119:113-116

¹¹³ I hate the double-minded,
   but I love *your law*.
¹¹⁴ You are my hiding place and my shield;
   I hope in *your word*.
¹¹⁵ Depart from me, you evildoers, that I
   may keep *the commandments of my God*.
¹¹⁶ Uphold me according to *your promise*,
   that I may live, and let me not be put to
   shame in my hope!

Reflection

There will never be a time when we have "all the information" we desire. All of the pieces of information, even if they were available, would be difficult to process in a coherent way. This challenge is what makes living without God even more difficult. Maybe even impossible.

God has promised that "for those who love God all things work together for good, for those who are called according to his purpose" (Romans 8:28). What this means is that in spite of our deficits, God is able to take all we do not know into account. Therefore, even when we miss things, and we will, God does not.

The question I ask myself is this: how do I enjoy the benefits of this promise? The Psalmist reminds us it is God's words, and our daily consumption of it, that reminds us of what we have and what we do not have to worry about any longer.

We can find comfort in the middle of all manner of difficult situations and circumstances because we can trust God to see us through. In this we can find an abiding peace and a steady flow of comfort.

Commentary

Verse 113: As a thought experiment, what would be the opposite of being "double-minded"? The implication of the phrase is that the person being labeled in this way is unreliable. They are not able to pick a path and stick with it. So, the opposite of being double-minded is being single-minded; being a person of resolve and conviction. The mistake we should avoid here is this, as followers of Christ the mind we seek to be resolved in is not our own. Rather, we should be single-minded in our resolve to do as God has commanded in his word. For it is there that God has revealed his mind to us. The apostle Paul writes it like this: "Let this mind be in you, which was also in Christ Jesus..." (Philippians 2:5 KJV). Our minds need renewal. Therefore, we should not place too much confidence in what our minds can conceive. It is not as trustworthy as we may like to believe.

Verse 114: One of the many benefits of studying and meditating on God's word is the peace it brings. Knowing who God is and how he has promised to work in our lives is a true blessing. We have to normalize the idea that the greatest miracle is not what we can get from God, but that God has already given us access to himself. He is our "hiding place and [our] shield."

Verse 115: As we journey through this life, we must be vigilant of those who would encourage us to deviate from God's purposes. In the simplest sense, these individuals are "evildoers." And why that seems harsh and unkind, not seeing them in this way causes us to drop our guard and to be blinded to the tactics being used against our faith. These evildoers would ask us to substitute what we have learned about God for what they claim to know about God. This should never be. As we keep God's commandments, we must grow in our resolve to dismiss those who would cause us to detour from where God is leading.

Verse 116: "Let me not be put to shame in my hope!" This is the call of a sincere heart. The mind of God is so much higher than ours. Because of this, we will not always understand everything God has asked us to do. In times like these we are to place our trust in God's faithfulness and goodness. We are living with the hope that God will "uphold [us] according to [his] promise."

This is what living by faith means. We obey and leave the outcomes to God.

Psalm 119:117-120

¹¹⁷ Hold me up, that I may be safe and have
regard for *your statutes* continually!
¹¹⁸ You spurn all who go astray from *your
statutes*, for their cunning is in vain.
¹¹⁹ All the wicked of the earth you
discard like dross, therefore
I love *your testimonies*.
¹²⁰ My flesh trembles for fear of you, and I
am afraid of *your judgments*.

Reflection

As the world continues to deal with and address the ramifications of a global pandemic, the words of Psalm 119 seem particularly useful. The uncertainty of the innumerable variables can cause us to feel unsteady in the world. This unbalanced feeling impacts how we make choices in every area of our lives.

When we find ourselves being buffeted by the waves of the circumstances we encounter in life, we need to find a fixed point that can guide us home, to safety. That north star is God's word for those of us who claim the name of Jesus. God's word is the guiding light in the darkness and unpredictability of the current state of the world. It can be difficult trying to make sense of what is happening when everything around us appears to be constant motion.

The Christian faith points to an eternal reality beyond the shores of life in this world. This perspective can and should give us comfort. It is the constant reminder that we are passing through. We do not need to take a morbid posture to the uncertainties of life. We should take the attitude that what happens here and now does not have the power to rob us of what is to come.

This is a key part of the eschatological hope of the Christian faith. We live today, enjoy today, and embrace today while we seek others to join us on this journey toward heaven. Through it all we do everything we can to keep our eyes pointed to Jesus. In him we have hope. In him we place our joy. In him we find direction to guide us and purpose to keep us moving. We do not look to the things of this world. At least this is the way it should be.

Commentary

Verse 117: Once we have experienced the grace of God, it is difficult to live without it. The beauty of God's love is we are not cast away when we falter and fail. God's goodness draws us back when we are sincere in our remorse. There are some who would say this is taking advantage of God's grace. That might be true, if the person's heart was to do as they wished. However, knowing we will sin and wanting to continue doing it are not the same. This difference matters and it matters to God. He is the one who knows the heart of the one who comes to him seeking to be restored and reconciled. And God promises to receive all who come with a contrite heart.

Verse 118: To adhere to God's statutes is to declare a trust in God's wisdom. To reject God's commands is to expose a lack of trust in God's care. As a result, when those who obey God's word experience blessings, they can make those who do not feel as if they have been rejected by God. This is not an intentional act of discipline by God, but the natural consequence of going one's own way, apart from God. When we separate ourselves from God, we will experience the consequences of no longer being under his divine protection.

Verse 119: One of the characteristics of many of the psalms is the personal and intimate tone they take. We see expressions of anger and desires for revenge in those places where the writer feels under attack. These emotions should not be interpreted in ways that diminish the human experience. However, they should also not be understood as endorsements by God about what the author desires or should expect by God. One of the simpler ways of understanding this kind of language is as an awareness by God of the difficulties that emerge in the human experience. In this light, the speaker in the psalms can describe what they perceive is happening, or even hope would happen, without imposing upon God some obligation foreign to his character.

Verse 120: When we find the word "fear" in the scriptures, it has become common to speak of a reverence and honoring of God. While in many cases the context would justify this understanding of the word, this is not one of those cases. There is a real sense in which the reality of God's "judgments" must be understood as terror inducing. The reason for this is an acknowledgement of the tremendous power and complete authority which God has to adjudicate sin. While it is proper to say God desires to dispense grace and mercy, God must also uphold his righteousness in the face of sin. Therefore, to fear God, in this context, is to recognize how bad it could be for us, if it were not for God's grace.

Psalm 119:121-124

¹²¹ I have done what is just and right; do
    not leave me to my oppressors.
¹²² Give your servant *a pledge of good*; let not
    the insolent oppress me.
¹²³ My eyes long for your salvation and for
    the fulfillment of *your righteous promise*.
¹²⁴ Deal with your servant according
    to your steadfast love, and teach
    me *your statutes*.

Reflection

God's faithfulness to his own promises may be the most powerful reason for trusting in God. To accept and live in the knowledge that God will do what he has said brings freedom and hope.

Disappointment can have such a crushing effect on us. It can distort our understanding of self. It can make us look at others in the worst possible light. Relationships can be forever ruined because of expectations that were not met. But how do we deal with expectations that were never really possible? Expectations that we created that were not based in truth?

This is why when I find myself being disappointed with God, I have to stop and ask: Is this something God said he would do? Or is this something that I want God to do, and because he didn't, I am now angry?

God will accomplish what he has promised. God will never accomplish what he has never promised. Both of these realities are comforting. The first because God can be trusted. The second because God cannot be manipulated.

Commentary

Verse 121: The witness of our lives is a plea with God to remember his promises. When we live in accord with God's character, we will reap the blessings that come with that. However, those who do not share our faith will find reason to come against us. In spite of this opposition, we can trust in God to safeguard us through the circumstances we face until we finally stand before him in heaven.

Verse 122: When God speaks, what he says must be accomplished. God has never promised anything he has failed to provide. This is what true divine faithfulness looks like. Just because we do not always understand how God is working does not mean that he is not active and engaged in the world and in our lives.

Verse 123: It is interesting to describe the longing for salvation in the context of "seeing". What makes this of particular interest is the way it helps us understand that whatever salvation is, it will be something that can be seen with the eye. What will be seen will be the fulfillment of what God has promised. What the Psalmist was waiting for we have seen in its fullness in Jesus.

Verse 124: God in his goodness will judge the world and discipline his children in a consistent manner. What this means is when God acts, he cannot be accused of wrongdoing. His faithfulness to his own character is what guarantees that justice will always be performed by God. Within this context, when we learn God's statutes, we can know the standard we will be measured against.

Psalm 119:125-128

¹²⁵ I am your servant; give me
  understanding, that I may
  know *your testimonies!*
¹²⁶ It is time for the Lord to act,
  for *your law* has been broken.
¹²⁷ Therefore I love *your commandments*
  above gold, above fine gold.
¹²⁸ Therefore I consider all *your precepts* to
  be right; I hate every false way.

Reflection

One of my favorite movies growing up was *The Karate Kid*. In that movie a young man, Daniel Larusso, moves across the country and has his life turned upside down. He moves to a new town, a different way of doing things, and with no one to help him navigate this new reality. Most people already know the arch of the story, so I will not rehash it here.

As Daniel meets Mr. Miyagi and begins his training, Daniel is asked to perform routine chores. He does not understand what any of these tasks have to do with learning karate. It is not until Daniel has gotten fed up with being treated like slave labor that the "lessons" are revealed. What the master knew, the pupil was now going to learn.

In the Christian life, context is key. Without context we will not properly understand what is happening around us. And whoever defines that context for us, will determine how we see what comes next.

In the tension between feeling used and being trained, we see the link between obedience and faith. Daniel thought he was being used and taken advantage of. Daniel thought that he had been lied to! But Mr. Miyagi knew something as well. He knew his pupil needed to have new patterns ingrained in his mind.

The repetition of the movements of washing cars, painting fences, and sanding floors were all in preparation for the revelation. And what was that revelation? That Daniel had learned more karate doing "non karate" things than he could have imagined.

Yes, the movie is an oversimplification of the years it takes for mastery. But it is a wonderful example of what happens when we obey our teacher and then, in a moment, we are awakened to the truth. We know and understand more than we thought, but we just didn't see it properly. We couldn't see it because we wanted it all to look like something else.

This, at its core, is discipleship. We obey those we trust in the faith. We follow and imitate their example.

And then, when we are ready, we begin to see what was right in front of us the whole time.

Commentary

Verse 125: As we surrender to God's instruction, we embrace a new direction for our lives. In this sense, we become servants of God. Not in an overbearing or hostile manner. But rather as a willing and appreciative response to God's grace. As we serve, we are invited to grow in our understanding. However, there are times where we reach the end of what we know, and so we ask for greater levels of insight. God desires for our wisdom to grow. Therefore, we should not be shy in asking for more of it.

Verse 126: We do not always understand God's timing. It can be difficult to see how much is being "overlooked" by God. So, when we have become familiar with God's law, our sense of indignation can at times get the better of us. We see something that is out of line, or someone that is flaunting their disobedience and we wonder, "Where is God?" The answer is, he is right where he has always been. God will act when he chooses. Not when we think he should.

Verse 127: In this verse, we see another instance where the Psalmist speaks of their love of God's commandments. While this sentiment would appear counter-intuitive, it is the attitude we should seek to cultivate. To understand what God's commandments are, and what they do, is to see how they are also expressions of God's affection and grace toward us. They will then become the most precious gifts in our lives. Or at least we may appreciate them more honestly.

Verse 128: To acknowledge the source of God's precepts, is to also accept that they cannot be wrong. This may be difficult to understand when we begin our journey of faith. However, to trust God is to trust what he has said. Understanding is, in the Christian life, the consequence of obedience. We do what God commands and then we learn why it is true. This is most often the pattern and process of deeper relationship with God.

Psalm 119:129-132

¹²⁹ *Your testimonies* are wonderful;
    therefore my soul keeps them.
¹³⁰ The unfolding of *your words* gives
    light; it imparts understanding
    to the simple.
¹³¹ I open my mouth and pant, because I
    long for *your commandments*.
¹³² Turn to me and be gracious to me,
    as is your way with those who love
    your name.

Reflection

The first verse in the selection points to the wonderful nature of God's testimonies. What makes these testimonies wonderful is we can participate in them. Throughout all of the events contained in the Bible, we are made witnesses to what God was doing in and through the circumstances recorded.

As we witness these moments and events, we are given a glimpse of how God works in the affairs of men. How God weaves his purposes through the faithful choices, and even acts of sin, of the various players. We see how God is able to take even the most unwise decisions and use them to advance his will.

The danger we face as we reflect on these events is failing to see the hand of God in the story. While the Bible contains the history of God's people, these stories are also a chronicle of God's own history with the world. From the opening majesty of creation that is described; to the glorious miracle of Jesus's resurrection from the grave; to the final triumphant victory by God over the devil at the end of the ages; all of these highlights and all of the moments in between are exposing the wonder of God in time and in the world.

We can often miss it because we become distracted by the everyday challenges of life. But we must find a way, from time to time, to pause and see how much wonder actually is all around us.

Commentary

Verse 129: The word of God is filled with wonderful realities. The stories that convey these truths can be difficult, even harsh. But, through them we can gain a glimpse of what God has been doing. The wonder of God's word can fill us. That is one of the main attributes of the entire process. We should not forget this. This wonder-inducing power of God's word is how we are drawn closer to God. Our soul's keep what can actually fill us with wonder.

Verse 130: The word of God is revelation from the mind of God. The totality of what it contains cannot be understood in one sitting. It will take a lifetime of study to even scratch the surface of all God has shared with us. However, the more time we spend with God's word, the more of it we understand. Not because we become wiser, even though that will happen. We understand more because the Holy Spirit illuminates our minds to receive what is there waiting to be learned. To grow in understanding takes time. Therefore, we should take the time to grow in our understanding. We should not feel like we have missed something, when we can reflect on how much we actually have acquired.

Verse 131: The longing described by the Psalmist here is telling. It not only describes a keen awareness of what God offers, but it exposes a knowledge of the value of what God provides. To receive and take in what God gives is to be truly satisfied. Only God can fill what our soul most desires. And the reason is simple. Only God has the infinite resources to accomplish the task.

Verse 132: For those who love the Lord, there is no need to fear about how God will treat us. When we have understood his grace and have experienced his mercy, our perception of what it means to serve God changes. The Psalmist describes this graciousness according to the surety of its continuation. The writer says, "as is your way." The reason we can know how God will act is not because we have figured God out. It is because God has revealed to us how he will act, and we can either trust or not. To trust is to enjoy the benefits of God's unchanging character.

Psalm 119:133-136

¹³³ Keep steady my steps according to *your promise*, and let no iniquity get dominion over me.
¹³⁴ Redeem me from man's oppression, that I may keep *your precepts*.
¹³⁵ Make your face shine upon your servant, and teach me *your statutes*.
¹³⁶ My eyes shed streams of tears, because people do not keep *your law*.

Reflection

Once you have tasted the goodness of God, it becomes difficult to forget what you have experienced. This is one of the more surprising aspects of the Christian journey. We can try and pretend we don't remember what God has done. However, we can never erase the memory of God's grace and goodness.

The longer I live, the more aware I become of what it means to believe the Gospel of Jesus Christ. The irony is that I am not saying I understand it better. As a matter of fact, I feel like it makes less sense. Not because I am confused, but because I understand exactly what it means!

God the Father made a plan with Jesus the Son to enter into the brokenness of this world. As a part of that plan they formulated a way for lost sinners to be redeemed from their fallen condition and be reconciled with God.

When you really think about it, that just doesn't make any sense. Why would God do that? And even more to the point, why would I believe that? The answer is both simple and overwhelming. It is simple because if we take God's word at face value, that he actually means what he has said, then we have to accept that his love is without reservation or boundary.

But, believing the Gospel is also overwhelming. It is so because to acknowledge God's action to save we have to accept how terrible our sin actually is. If the cross of Calvary is what it took to save lost sinners, how could we not want others to know and enjoy this love with us?

Commentary

Verse 133: As we walk the journey of faith, the opportunities to stumble do not decrease. They may very well increase. It does not matter in which direction it is, as long as we keep walking towards God's will, we can trust in God's direction. This is the request here. "Keep steady my steps." An honest prayer for a certain reality in this world.

Verse 134: The life of faithful obedience will have a cost. That cost, most often, manifests itself in the opposition of those who do not live with a similar conviction. Submission to God's commands will identify us and mark us for greater scrutiny. Whether that evaluation leads to blessing or hardship cannot be determined beforehand. Each person we encounter in life must choose how they will respond to our faith. But regardless of their choice, we must continue to keep God's precepts.

Verse 135: In a poetic sense, almost all references to God's face is an acknowledgment of an intimate relationship with God. To see God's face or to speak to God face-to-face is to connect with how God referred to his relationship with Moses. This is what we should aspire to. This is why the link between the request for God to make his face "shine upon your servant" and God's statutes is interesting. The implication seems to be that the more intimate our relationship with God, the greater our receptivity to God's commands.

Verse 136: The Psalmist laments how so many others fail to keep God's law. The sadness comes from a keen awareness of all the writer has enjoyed as a result of accepting the revelation of God's wisdom. To see others deny themselves of this, either by ignorance or by choice, is a deeply troubling realization. One that calls us to embrace a greater witness, not a timid retreat.

Psalm 119:137-140

¹³⁷ Righteous are you, O Lord,
 and right are *your rules*.
¹³⁸ You have appointed *your testimonies* in
 righteousness and in all faithfulness.
¹³⁹ My zeal consumes me, because my foes
 forget *your words*.
¹⁴⁰ *Your promise* is well tried, and your
 servant loves it.

Reflection

It is difficult to trust in God's word when we do not always trust in God. I am not sure what other conclusion we can draw.

If we say we believe the Scriptures are God's revelation to humanity, but we do not seek to understand its meaning or conform our lives to its mandates, questions must be asked. Do we actually believe what we claim?

One of the initial challenges to the Christian life is accepting the whole of God's word as God's word. To begin to grapple with all that the sacred texts contain. To consider where our lives are not in alignment with the example and expectations of God's character as it is revealed in Scripture.

The life of faith is not merely about performing rote functions at religious meetings. This is not what God desires or expects from us. However, if we do not honestly engage with the wisdom God has provided in the Bible, but rather find reasons and ways of explaining away what is there, we will not find our faith in God growing. It will have been sabotaged before it even has a chance to get up to speed.

Commentary

Verse 137: The righteousness of God is what instills within us confidence in the rightness of the rules he gives to us. When we know God has commanded us to do something, we do not have to question whether we should do it. By virtue of it having been given by God, we should proceed with urgency.

Verse 138: What God has said will not be overturned. There is nothing that can do it. And there is no one who has the authority to do it. God's word is unchangeable for God himself is unchanging. While this should cause us concern regarding our fellow human beings, we ought not have any such fears related to God. Human nature can be fickle and erratic. Therefore, we all must strive to grow, mature, and improve. God's nature has no such flaws or shortcomings. For this we can be ever thankful.

Verse 139: To be zealous, is to have a deep and constant passion for something. In this verse we see the zeal of the writer is overwhelming. They look at what is happening to those who forget the words of God and are motivated to redouble their efforts. To truly know God's word is to become passionate about all it instructs.

Verse 140: When a child of God takes God at his word, the result is a fulfilled promise. The Psalmist tells us they have tested God's promises and they have been found firm and unimpeachable. When our confidence in God is reaffirmed over and over again, it is difficult to lose hope or become distracted by the many trials and temptations of life. God's faithful fulfillment of his promises gives us all the more reason to rejoice in God.

Psalm 119:141-144

¹⁴¹ I am small and despised, yet I do not
   forget *your precepts*.
¹⁴² Your righteousness is righteous forever,
   and *your law* is true.
¹⁴³ Trouble and anguish have found
   me out, but *your commandments*
   are my delight.
¹⁴⁴ *Your testimonies* are righteous forever;
   give me understanding that I may live.

Reflection

Of the many attributes of the psalms in the Bible, one that I greatly appreciate is the honesty we find there. The sharing of private thoughts and fears, of the struggles and frustrations of life. There are few emotions that are not explored. And some of them are uncomfortably raw.

But life is like this. So many of our private thoughts never find expression. As a result, they are buried and can have a negative effect on our minds and hearts. The regular reading of the Psalms is a practice we should all take up.

One of the oddities of life is how little we are able to express, without judgment, some of the darker thoughts we have. We need to cultivate a habit of honest confession with a trusted friend. The idea is not to burden another person with our struggles, but to share our burdens with one another. In the process, we learn to live together in the hills and valleys of life's journey.

It can be scary to be this honest. But God is neither afraid nor ashamed of hearing about the deep hurts and worries we have. We should therefore do all we can to be as honest as God allows.

Commentary

Verse 141: As the days and years of life accrue, the opportunities to be reminded of our condition apart from God increase. We are lost without God. We have no real reason for eternal hope if we do not fellowship with God. However, when we have been reconciled to God; when we have experienced the grace of God in the cross of Christ; when we have been filled and empowered by the Holy Spirit, our frailty is no longer an obstacle. Our reception of God's precepts gives us the ballast we need so we do not succumb to the tempests of life.

Verse 142: The writer calls us to ponder: How long will God's goodness last? While the question may appear nonsensical, how we answer it matters. God will be good for as long as God is God. This is axiomatically true. So, what does that say about God's law? It says that as long as

God is God, his law shall be true. God's character is the guarantee of his law's veracity and longevity.

Verse 143: In the midst of the toils of life, it is good to have a safe harbor in which to rest. God's commandments have not always been seen in this light. However, the implication of the Psalmist's joy in spite of the trials of life should give us pause. To delight in God's commandments does not require a trouble free life. It does require us to put our focus on the gift of God's word and see it as it truly is.

Verse 144: The testimonies of God shall be good and for our good as long as God lives. What a glorious truth. Our confidence in living according to what God commands is not in our ability to execute what God says, but in trusting God to lead us into greater understanding and deeper commitment.

Psalm 119:145-148

¹⁴⁵ With my whole heart I cry; answer me,
   O Lord! I will keep *your statutes*.
¹⁴⁶ I call to you; save me, that I may
   observe *your testimonies*.
¹⁴⁷ I rise before dawn and cry for help;
   I hope in *your words*.
¹⁴⁸ My eyes are awake before the
   watches of the night, that I may
   meditate on *your promise*.

Reflection

When I initially wrote this reflection, we were right in the middle of Holy Week. I was reminded of how ill-prepared the disciples must have felt they were for what was about to happen. The difficulties they were about to face were many. And most of them were nowhere on the horizon in their minds.

I find it interesting to see how they were able to rebound. How in spite of the challenges and the fears, they were able to enter into the mission Jesus sent them on. I do not have a naive view of the situation. It's just that when I look at all that happened, the reality of Jesus's resurrection restored their hope and renewed their strength.

It is a rare occurrence where we know what will happen in life. Sometimes we can have a good idea of what will happen. If we are honest, most of the time, we are just doing the best we can with the information we have available. There are so many uncertainties we cannot even begin to imagine or calculate.

That is why being grounded in God's word is so helpful to living in this world. God has given us some tools for living well. Those tools provide us a way of countering the downward pull of sin and hopelessness. But we have to receive this wisdom from above. We have to trust it. We have to put it into practice.

The disciples of Pentecost were the same disciples of Good Friday. They just had some new information. What Jesus said had become what God did. This shift is so important to live lives that are pleasing to God and satisfactory to ourselves.

Commentary

Verse 145: We should approach God with a sincere heart. Not with half-hearted measures. To seek the counsel of God with our whole heart is key to our faith journey. Why? Because when we fully commit to this pursuit, we can know that God was the one who came through. We did not put our trust in ourselves, but in God.

Verse 146: If we desire to be living witnesses of God's grace, we desire a good thing. The writer shares their desire for deliverance so that they might continue in service to God. Our service to God can be both an opportunity for glorifying God, but also a time where we see the word of God come to life in us.

Verse 147: The discipline of taking time throughout the day for focused attention on God's word is not new. It is a practice that has been around for a long time. There has been much discussion over what time of the day this activity should be done. Here the Psalmist suggests that before the dawn of a new day is good. A practical reason for this early allocation of time is it precedes all other activity in the day.

Verse 148: Continuing on the theme of the previous verse, the Psalmist reiterates the practice of early meditation on God's promise. Remembering and reflecting on the promises of God is a good way of orienting our days. This kind of perspective can have a calming effect on our minds when we know of specific challenges, we have to face in the hours to come.

Psalm 119:149-152

¹⁴⁹ Hear my voice according to your
    steadfast love; O Lord, according to
    your justice give me life.
¹⁵⁰ They draw near who persecute me with
    evil purpose; they are far from *your law*.
¹⁵¹ But you are near, O Lord, and all *your
    commandments* are true.
¹⁵² Long have I known from *your testimonies*
    that you have founded them forever.

Reflection

When we approach God, an important consideration is whether we understand how God has revealed he will act. The reason we have to keep this in mind is when we do not we run the risk of mischaracterizing who God is. When God says, "This is who I am," we should take God at his word.

God's character is what God says it is. Not what I wish it was. That means if God does anything contrary to his character, he could be accused of being a liar. And if

God is a liar, then he cannot be trusted. And if God cannot be trusted, then he is not worthy of worship or allegiance.

Our study of God through his word is one of the surest ways we have to better understand how we build our relationship with God. When we do not know what God has done or what God has said, we cannot really know how we should behave around God.

The longer I live, the more I think about this. If I want to know God, I have to take what God has said about himself more seriously. I have to hold God's "feet to the fire" so to speak. And God is not afraid of my approaching him on these terms.

Commentary

Verse 149: The Psalmist pleads with God to hear and to give them life according to God's love and justice. These two realities are the ultimate expressions of God's grace. We are loved like a child by a good father, and we are shown mercy when what we deserve is wrath from a holy judge. The tension these realities create could only be reconciled by God. This is why they should inspire awe and give us the courage to request both from God.

Verse 150: Our distance from God's law is an indication of what we are capable of if left to our own devices. This is true in us, and it is true in those who seek to do us harm. The language of persecution reveals the intensity of the opposition. When we are under such attack we must remember the promises of God's word as they are expressed in God's law.

Verse 151: The Psalmist has expressed several times that the veracity of God's commandments can be best seen in our nearness to God. This nearness is not a physical proximity. What is being described is a nearness of character. As we are conformed to God's character, we see more clearly why what God says is true. This verse is also an extension of the thought in the previous verse. Particularly in the idea that our nearness to God is a blessing to us, but for those who persecute us, the distance distorts their moral compass.

Verse 152: What God has revealed will never fail and cannot be revoked. This is the simplest way of understanding the writer's idea here. The reason? Because they are grounded in God's own being. "You founded them forever" connects what God says with who God is, as we have seen before.

Psalm 119:153-156

¹⁵³ Look on my affliction and deliver me,
   for I do not forget *your law*.
¹⁵⁴ Plead my cause and redeem me; give me
   life according to *your promise!*
¹⁵⁵ Salvation is far from the wicked, for
   they do not seek *your statutes*.
¹⁵⁶ Great is your mercy, O Lord; give me life
   according to *your rules*.

Reflection

For the people of God, the miracle of holy writ serves as the foundation of faith and life. Without God's wisdom codified, we will have a difficult time transitioning to God's wisdom personified.

If we desire to live in a manner worthy of God's love, we have to understand what God's love creates in us. What I do not mean is that we are trying to earn God's favor, as if by good works. But we, recognizing the beauty of God's free gift, want to do all we can to show our appreciation to God. We live now in response to God's grace.

These realities do not need to be confused. We can live in obedience, but not in an effort to manipulate God. And we can live in a posture of thankfulness, and not take what God has done for granted. We may feel there is a tension between these realities, but that is because of our struggles to do them, not because there is any contradiction between them.

If we could recapture the balance and the tension of this, we may well understand what has been missing in the Church in recent years. Our efforts to simplify have become oversimplifications. There is a difference. And not knowing how these are different can be hazardous to our faith and the health of the body of Christ.

As the old hymn captured it: "Trust and obey, for there's no other way / to be happy in Jesus, but to trust and obey."[3]

Commentary

Verse 153: There have been several instances in the psalm where the effect of affliction has been tied to not forgetting God's law. The implication of this theme is that when we are under duress, our initial inclination will be to abandon what God has commanded believing this will bring relief from what is causing us pain. This tendency must be anticipated and it should not be a surprise when this feeling emerges. Remembering God's

---

[3] https://hymnary.org/text/when_we_walk_with_the_lord

word is an important discipline to develop before times of great stress and difficulty.

Verse 154: The kind of life we live will be impacted by the many choices we make in life. If those choices are made without the counsel of God and the wisdom of his word, we put ourselves at risk. As we grow in our understanding of God's promises, we can better appreciate the life God is leading us to live. Over the course of our lives, we become more sensitive to the Holy Spirit's work in us. This increased sensitivity is what supports and fortifies our trust in God's direction.

Verse 155: The Psalmist points to the relationship between salvation of the soul and obedience to God's statutes. It should not be said that obedience guarantees salvation. That is not the direction of the text. Rather, the lack of obedience reveals that an individual has not reckoned honoring God's commands as worthy of their efforts. This lack of submission indicates an absence of relationship. Without a relationship with God there can be no salvation. So, according to the author, our seeking of God's statutes serves as a barometer of what we believe about God and our relationship to him.

Verse 156: This refrain of "give me life" happens several times in the Psalm and twice in this selection of verses. It is an acknowledgment of God's unique place as the source of true life. This call from the Psalmist to God is instructive. By connecting the power of God to give life to the rules of God (and all the other synonymous phrases used), we can see how God uses his word to cultivate our faith and hope in him. What God says leads us to know who God is and what he has done for our redemption. All of this leads to the life God desires for his children.

Psalm 119:157-160

¹⁵⁷ Many are my persecutors and my
   adversaries, but I do not swerve from
   your testimonies.
¹⁵⁸ I look at the faithless with
   disgust, because they do not
   keep *your commands*.
¹⁵⁹ Consider how I love *your precepts*!
   Give me life according to your
   steadfast love.
¹⁶⁰ The sum of *your word* is truth,
   and every one of your *righteous
   rules* endures forever.

Reflection

On the Sunday before Jesus's arrest, trial, and crucifixion he entered the City of David for the final time. In a few short days, the earthly sojourn of the Son of God would come to an end and he would achieve his purpose.

The redemption of humanity was a task only God could accomplish. In the span of three years, Jesus of Nazareth went from obscurity to notoriety. Those who loved him, saw the hope of the world. Those who despised him, saw an interloper in their plans. Those who misunderstood him, betrayed him. Those who hated him, sought to kill him.

How could Jesus do it? How could he enter the city knowing what was to come? The question confounds us because if Jesus knew what we knew would happen, we would do everything in our power to escape. Not Jesus.

Jesus was not a prophet like Jonah, who ran in the other direction.

Jesus was not a king like David, who stayed home when he should go to fight.

Jesus was not a man like me, weak and timid in the face of great challenges.

We know the struggle of the Mount of Olives would come. We know that the request for reprieve would be made. The scriptures give us a glimpse into the events of those final days.

But we also know the surrender of obedience was perfectly fulfilled. Jesus's death on Friday would give way to his resurrection on Sunday morning.

We have the benefit of looking back. Of seeing across the pages of Scripture the events unfolding like a perfect drama.

However, few knew then what we know now. In truth, only Jesus knew what awaited him. Only Jesus.

This is the challenge of Palm Sunday. And it is the beauty of it as well. When we second guess God, we pretend to know more than we do, and to be better equipped to address the challenges we face.

Commentary

Verse 157: The challenges of life would rob us of the will to hold fast to God's testimonies, if we let them. We must not surrender to them. In the midst of struggle and strife, of challenges and challengers, we must continue being resolved to what we have seen and come to know about God.

Verse 158: In one of the more raw expressions in the psalm, we see the rancor of the Psalmist toward those who have rejected God's commands. Why does he feel this disdain? We cannot be sure. However, we can make a comparison. Based on the writer's love for and trust in God's word, we can catch a glimpse of the value he places on it. So, to see others not valuing what the Psalmist perceives as being of infinite worth causes feelings of disgust to rise in the writer. This is the kind of passion we should cultivate for God's word.

Verse 159: As a continuation of the previous verse's sentiments, we see a clear declaration of love for the precepts of God. We again see an admonition for God to give the Psalmist life according to God's steadfast love. This is the basis of the writer's confidence. There is no other reason for either making the request or expecting an answer. If God's love is not present, life will not flow toward us.

Verse 160: Every word of God is truth. What is interesting about the phrasing here is that "truth" is in the singular. The totality of God's revelation can be seen as one unified whole. This is an important perspective as it forces us to reevaluate how we interact with the Scriptures. In one sense they are a library of texts. But, in another, more profound way, they are one text. The interplay between these ideas is vital to a healthy understanding of God's revelation. We are not at liberty to pick and choose what we want to believe. We accept it all, or nothing at all.

Psalm 119:161-164

¹⁶¹ Princes persecute me without cause, but
my heart stands in awe of *your words*.
¹⁶² I rejoice at *your word* like one
who finds great spoil.
¹⁶³ I hate and abhor falsehood,
but I love *your law*.
¹⁶⁴ Seven times a day I praise you for
your righteous rules.

Reflection

Every year we celebrate what is commonly called Holy Week. During that time, the people of God enter one of the most important times of celebration in the Christian faith. What makes this week important is it affords us an intentional opportunity to remember the gift of salvation we have been given.

In the busyness of life, we can become quite distracted. The number of things that draw our attention from our faith can be overwhelming. Not that all of them are evil or sinful. The problem we have is we find it hard to refocus back on what God is calling us to.

This is why I appreciate the season of Lent in the weeks leading up to Easter. It is a time of preparation. But it also affords me the space to consider what takes up too much time in my life.

The discipline of taking stock of our lives is one we should not take for granted. In fact, we should take advantage of these times in the year when we can look at what we are doing and make important decisions. Decisions about what we want to change or adjust to maintain our focus on Jesus and our spiritual growth.

Commentary

Verse 161: The source of persecution may take the form of officials in high places, but even then, the admonition is to stay true to God's word. Here we see the Psalmist describe this commitment as "awe." There is something inspiring about God's word. It is simple enough for a child to read and yet profound enough to keep our attention for years. The depth of God's word is miraculous.

Verse 162: To see the word of God as a treasure is one of the best ways of thinking about it. The imagery here is that of discovery. The writer is minding their own business and comes upon the "great spoil" of God's word. One option is to ignore what you have found. But, when you know the value of what you now have before you, it is difficult not to rejoice. It is difficult to not do all you can to protect what you have found.

Verse 163: The law of God is juxtaposed with falsehood. This means the word of God is the measure of all claims. Or at least it should be. If what we are being told is not consistent or congruent with God's word, then we have to be cautious in entertaining it. We cannot live in accord with God's purposes if we are adopting falsehoods as a part of our lives. The truth and a lie cannot coexist.

Verse 164: Thankfulness for God's gracious gift of his word is an everyday event. We should never take our access to God's word for granted. The phrase "seven times a day" is a poetic way of saying continually. There ought not be an end to our appreciation for all God has revealed to us. It is a well that will never run dry, and we should praise God in response to his goodness in giving his word to us.

Psalm 119:165-168

¹⁶⁵ Great peace have those who love *your law*; nothing can make them stumble.
¹⁶⁶ I hope for your salvation, O Lord, and I do *your commandments.*
¹⁶⁷ My soul keeps *your testimonies*; I love them exceedingly.
¹⁶⁸ I keep *your precepts and testimonies,* for all my ways are before you.

Reflection

The Scriptures are not merely a collection of writings over the course of 1,600 centuries. They are more than that. The Old and New Testaments are the living record of God to his people. They are the testimonies of God's work in, and through, and sometimes even in spite of his people.

To not see the hand of God in his word is to not see God at all. I know that may appear to be a stretch to some. However, to reduce the Bible to simply the writings of men is to strip God completely away from his own word.

As Christians, we already believe fantastic things in order to be saved. Why do we then struggle to believe that the Bible is God's word and that what God has said in those writings can be dismissed or ignored? It defies any reason or consistency to do so.

Let us trust in God and let us trust in his word. Let us give thanks to God and let us give thanks for his word. Let us live for God and let us live out his word.

Commentary

Verse 165: To walk in alignment with God's word is to have a confidence and peace not available to others. The reason is not smugness or self-assurance. To walk in God's word is to walk in God's wisdom. Knowing this brings peace. There is no reason to fear what may come our way because we can call upon God for wisdom and aid.

Verse 166: There is no tension or contradiction between trusting in God to save and walking in obedience to God. As a matter of fact, the Psalmist seems to imply that this is the exact relationship between these two realities. To have hope in God to redeem is not antithetical to living our lives in submission to God's commands. When we learn this, we will be free to enjoy the wonder of God's love and the reward of sincere obedience.

Verse 167: God's word is spiritual. This is something we do not always remember. But it is something we should strive to remind ourselves of. While what God says may be enacted through physical activity, the true purpose is to conform us into the image of Jesus Christ. This transformation is one of the primary goals of our redemption. Also, because the word of God is of a spiritual nature, we can appreciate its worth by how it draws us to a deeper affection for them. As our love for God's word grows so will our love for God. For they point to him and reveal him to us.

Verse 168: Nothing we do escapes God's gaze. Therefore, we are better off to live our lives keeping God's "precepts and testimonies." To do anything different is to deny the place of God's word in our lives, and by extension God himself.

Psalm 119:169-172

¹⁶⁹ Let my cry come before you,
    O Lord; give me understanding
    according to *your word*!
¹⁷⁰ Let my plea come before you;
    deliver me according to *your word*.
¹⁷¹ My lips will pour forth praise,
    for you teach me *your statutes*.
¹⁷² My tongue will sing of *your word*,
    for all *your commandments* are right.

Reflection

The word of God is the great treasure of the Church. It is the message of hope for the lost and it is the perfect guide for those journeying towards heaven.

In the Scriptures we are given wisdom and counsel for living a righteous life. We are shown how to become angry and not sin, how to mourn and not lose hope.

As we turn the pages of our bibles we are able to witness the miraculous works of God even among the foolishness of broken people.

On virtually every page, the fullness of human frailty is on display. But right alongside this inadequacy we find the eternal strength of God.

The tapestry of history has been woven together by the steady hand of the God of heaven. Although the finished product escapes our understanding, we can trust in the vision and direction of the one who is weaving all things together.

Commentary

Verse 169: When we cry out to the Lord, we are expressing the deep needs of our hearts. In those moments we are seeking what only God can provide. While we all would like to be relieved of all the troubles of this world, there is something more important than the absence of pain. Living according to truth is vital to a life that pleases God and satisfies us. Therefore, what we need most of all, especially in times of difficulty is to understand what God is teaching us through his word. This kind of wisdom is clarifying and comforting, especially in times of strife.

Verse 170: As children of God, we can petition the Lord. He has given us access to his presence. This access is a precious gift, and one we can enjoy often. When we bring to God our cares, we must accept the deliverance he extends. We can become discouraged when God does not act according to our desires. But our desires do not compare to the infinite wisdom of God.

Verse 171: A grateful heart will give thanks for God's instruction. Not because we liked what we were being taught, but because we were being taught by God. Not every lesson is easy. Sometimes the lessons we must face are difficult and costly. But if God is the teacher, then the reward is worth the price and the effort.

Verse 172: Not only is thankfulness an appropriate response to God's faithfulness to his word, so is singing. When we sing, we are engaging not just the rational faculties of the mind, but also the emotional realities of the soul. The "right"-ness of God's word only increases our confidence and joy when we sing.

Psalm 119:173-176

¹⁷³ Let your hand be ready to help me, for I
have chosen *your precepts*.
¹⁷⁴ I long for your salvation, O Lord,
and *your law* is my delight.
¹⁷⁵ Let my soul live and praise you,
and let *your rules* help me.
¹⁷⁶ I have gone astray like a lost sheep;
seek your servant, for I do not
forget *your commandments*.

Reflection

As we conclude our study through Psalm 119, I wanted to take a little time and look at what we have learned. The author of this psalm wanted to look at and extol the wonders, beauty, and majesty of God's word. The synonyms and images used to describe God's revelation have been many. And the implications are just as varied.

First, God's word is not just for religious exercise. Engaging and consuming God's word has very practical ramifications for how we live in the world and with others. To know how to live well, we need the best information and insights we can get. There is no greater wisdom than that given by God. Therefore, we should seek it, meditate on it, and employ it in our daily living.

Second, God's word is a source of comfort. The constant reminder of God's faithfulness and goodness are found throughout God's word. We are given encouragement to remember the grace and mercy of God; to be called to deep trust and truer affection of God as we read and consider the history recorded. For that history is one that weaves together the affairs of men and the will of God in the world.

Third, God's word is a library of instruction. God desires for his people to know how to live in a way that reflects his character. In order to achieve this, we have to learn what is in line with God's character and what is not. As we study God's word, we can see what he commands. As we grow in our obedience, we are transformed. As we are transformed, we become more like Jesus, who is our example of a God-filled life.

Finally, God's word is a promissory note. What God has promised he will fulfill. To do anything less is for God to open the door to accusations of being a liar. God will comply with every promise he makes, and he makes no promise he cannot fulfill. This is the beauty of God's love. He can do what he says. Just because we would have done things differently does not mean God has failed. It should help us realize there are still things we do not know.

God's word is the anchor for our faith. When we go to it, we can find the God who gave us those words. But we have to be looking for him there to find him.

Commentary

Verse 173: The phrasing of the verse leaves the impression that the Psalmist, by choosing God's precepts, is "reminding" God of what God has promised. Now, God does not need reminders. And that is not really the intent. The author is not putting an artificial demand upon God. Rather, the author is acknowledging the reality of what God has promised to do when a believer lives in obedience to what God commands.

Verse 174: When we have come to know what God has said, our desire for salvation intensifies. What this would suggest is not that the gift of salvation has been rescinded and then reapplied. God's promise to keep us will never be at risk of being undone. What we see here is that our delight in God's law is a steady reminder to us. It is a reminder that all who believe in Jesus are the beneficiaries of this great salvation that will never be taken away.

Verse 175: The writer describes the posture of life they are taking. They want to live in such a way that it is obvious to all who see they are committed to God with the totality of their being. For the soul to "live and praise" God means that in daily living there will be an element of worship. That in all things God will be glorified.

Verse 176: The final verse of the psalm is a bit odd. The oddity is that after all the various ways the Psalmist describes and rejoices in God's faithfulness to keep them, they end on a note of deep humility. This acknowledgment of a tendency to fail in keeping God's commands serves two purposes. First, it is a humble admonition that wandering away from God is not only possible, but far more likely than we would like to admit. Therefore, we should take care and be mindful. So, a petition is made for God to seek out the wandering sheep. Second, through this humble declaration we can see we can trust in God's faithfulness to seek us when we wander and to never abandon us when we feel like we have disappointed God. Even when we drift (or even run) off course, we can remember what we have learned about God. And it is this knowledge that will help us find our way back home.

Author Page

Victor R. Scott currently serves as the Executive Pastor for Ministry Development and Discipleship at Ambassadors of Christ Ministries in Columbus, Georgia. He is also the General Overseer for the Diocese of Columbus as well as the Executive Director of Policy and Procedure for Alliance Partners Network International.

He graduated from Georgia Southern University with his undergraduate degree and completed his Master of Divinity degree from Luther Rice University and Seminary.

Victor married his high school sweetheart and they have two daughters who happen to share the same birthday.

To find out more about Victor and find more reading material you can go to his website.

www.VictorScott.org

www.ingramcontent.com/pod-product-compliance
Lightning Source LLC
Chambersburg PA
CBHW072021060426
42449CB00033B/1415